Hélène Gingold

Seven Stories

Second Edition

Hélène Gingold

Seven Stories
Second Edition

ISBN/EAN: 9783337005221

Printed in Europe, USA, Canada, Australia, Japan

Cover: Foto ©Thomas Meinert / pixelio.de

More available books at **www.hansebooks.com**

SEVEN STORIES.

BY
HÉLÈNE E. A. GINGOLD.

The world's all title page : there's no contents ;
The world's all face : the man who shows his heart
Is hooted for his nudities, and scorn'd.
Young's Night Thoughts.

SECOND EDITION.

REMINGTON AND CO., LIMITED,
LONDON AND SYDNEY.
MDCCCXCIII.

TO MY UNCLE,

BARON NICOLA NISCO OF SAINT GIORGIO LA MONTAGNA,

Senator, Deputy, and Historian Royal of Italy,

THIS HUMBLE VOLUME IS AFFECTIONATELY AND RESPECTFULLY DEDICATED BY

THE AUTHOR.

NOTE.

The subjoined letter, a translation of which appears on the page next following, is one of which I may claim to be justly gratified. In expressing gratification at being the recipient of such flattering sentiments, let me also hasten to add that it is not because they emanate from a Royal personage, but because they are the thoughts of one who has gained a world-wide reputation in the field of Art and Literature.

Geb.-Cabinet
Sr. Hoheit des Herzogs
von
S. COBURG-GOTHA.

Coburg,

Hochgeehrtes Fräulein!

Im Höchsten Auftrag beehre ich mich Ihnen mitzutheilen, daß Seine Hoheit der Herzog von Ihren anziehenden Dichtungen mit freundlichem Interesse Kenntniß genommen hat und namentlich das Talent anerkennt, das in den realistisch gehaltenen Sittenschilderungen Ihres Romans zu Tage tritt Seine Hoheit ist Ihnen für die liebenswürdige Form, in der Sie die Erzeugnisse Ihrer Muse Höchstdemselben dargeboten haben, aufrichtig dankbar, und als ein Zeichen Seiner wohlgeneigten Gesinnung Ihnen die beiliegende Photographie Seiner Hoheit zu übersenden.

Mit vorzüglicher Hochachtung

DR. TEMPLETEY.

(TRANSLATION.)

GEH.-CABINET
SR. HOHEIT DES HERZOGS
VON
S. COBURG GOTHA.

COBURG.

HIGHLY ESTEEMED MISS GINGOLD,

By command of H.H. the Duke of Saxe Coburg Gotha, I have much pleasure in informing you that H.H. has accepted and read with the greatest interest your charming book of poems. H.H. especially and fully recognises the descriptive and highly realistic talent evinced in your novel.

Further H.H. sincerely and gratefully thanks you for the charming manner with which your works were tendered to him.

I am further commissioned by H.H. to send you his accompanying photograph and autograph as a mark of the high esteem and consideration evinced by H.H. for your works.

Pray accept the marks of my highest consideration.

DR. TEMPLETEY.

PREFACE.

So often have I had the pleasure of addressing my friends, the Public, that it would appear that I am well used to it. But indeed such is not entirely the case. For, although an actor may, after a while, play a certain rôle with assurance, hey presto! his courage all flies when he is facing a critical audience for the first time in a new character. My former works have had such a favourable reception that I have been emboldened to take a novel departure (for me) and publish a series of what I call " SEVEN STORIES." Thus I stand before the curtain, the apprehensive actor in a new play, not yet knowing how my efforts will be received. It has been the custom since time immemorial for authors to say something of

Preface.

their work in the Preface, and from this time-honoured usage I shall not depart, although I intend my remarks shall be as brief as possible. One of my reasons for publishing this volume is, that it has appeared to me that short stories are required just as much as long ones. There is many a hard-worked man, aye, and woman too, who, on being asked if they have read this or that novel, answer deprecatingly (of themselves) "Well, no! The story is not a short one, and I haven't the time." These are people busy in the world of "Kunst und Wissenschaft," Members of Parliament, Doctors, Lawyers, Theologians, etc. Stories are written for the children of men, novels are written for those who have much time on their hands. But what of those sons and daughters of Earth whose every hour is precious, and who have little to spend on novel reading? For these especially I have written my Seven Short Stories, seeing that they are neglected by the rest of writers. It may be argued that my intentions are better than my work. To this I reply that I did my best, and that not to instruct and enlighten, but to amuse, and if I succeed in diverting the work-harrassed brain, be it but

Preface.

for one short hour, I well know that these humble stories have not been written in vain. I claim no especial distinction or inspiration for my book, only that I wrote more with Nature than with Art.

INDEX.

PAGE.

1. THE RABBI OF MOSCOW. (A Story of Two Religions.) - - - -   3

2. VERITAS. (A Metaphysical Story.) -   29

3. HOW TOM BELLAMY WON MY LORD HERTFORD'S WAGER. (An Olden-Time Sporting Story.) - - -   61

4. THE WHITE PRIEST. (A Ghost Story.)   93

5. WHOSE WAS THE GUILT? (The Story of a Social Problem.) - - -   133

6. THE DYING PROFESSOR. (A True Story.) - - - - -   147

7. THE TWO BROTHERS. (A Story of the Crusades.) - - - - -   155

THE RABBI OF MOSCOW.

I am a Jew. Hath not a Jew eyes? hath not a Jew hands, organs, dimensions, senses, affections, passions? fed with the same food, hurt with the same weapons, subject to the same diseases, warmed and cooled by the same winter and summer, as a Christian is?
Merchant of Venice.

THE RABBI OF MOSCOW.

A STORY OF LONG AGO, BUT WHICH MAY DO FOR TO-DAY.

"Trim the lamp, my Leah; and prythee, my dearly beloved grandchild, bring thy lute hither, for my heart to-night is fraught with some strange foreboding of impending ill, which thy sweet voice alone may serve to dispel."

The speaker was an old man of reverend aspect, whose snowy beard swept his breast, as did his locks his broad but slightly stooping shoulders. His countenance, at once noble and benign, was such as not years of oppression and suffering could alter in expression. All that remained of the fire of his youth, showed itself in his black, penetrating eyes, which also bore somewhat of the look of the hunted animal in their rapid glances.

No small wonder this, for he was one of the accursed race, without the power of following his belief, as even the idol worshipper may. He had been driven—he and his community—from place to place, and now he feared to be exiled again, for he wished to end his days in peace, where he had already been permitted to dwell for five years. His grand-daughter was all that remained of his family. His wife had died years before, leaving him an only daughter, and this one had married an honourable and wealthy Jew. But wealth and honour were nought—he was a Jew, and that was enough to brand him. The fiat went forth. The Jews must fly the country. Leah's mother succumbed in the snow with many others, and her husband shortly afterwards followed her to the grave—a poor heartbroken exile. For he had not been allowed time to collect his property. But the iron-built Rabbi remained to take charge of the infant grandchild, and he reared her as gently as the dove, yet instilling also into her mind the pride and lofty aspirations of the young eaglet. Beautiful, and full of affection for her old kinsman, the youthful Jewess exerted herself to render the thorny path of the Rabbi less hard and bitter.

This it was in her power to do, by singing to him such melodies as seemed the echoes of lost Jerusalem, and which were like a healing salve to his wounded spirit.

That night Leah seemed, too, in a sorrowful frame of mind; for, as she sat on a silken cushion at the old man's feet, she sang the following:

LEAH'S SONG.

I.

By the rivers of Babylon, captives, we wept,
   As a child by its mother forgot;
And grief, like an ocean, o'er us swept,
   For Zion, lov'd Zion, was not!

II.

We hang'd our harps on the willow-tree boughs,
   They bid us to sing, but in vain,
For who, unto song, their hearts can arouse,
   When bound in captivity's chain.

III.

Driven like brutes, from strand unto strand,
   Our minds e'en as fetter'd as we,
O! give back the land, we call our dear land,
   Where we may still reverence thee!

IV.

These climes our lov'd melodies ne'er shall know,
   Their words were not writ for the slave,
For us, hapless Israel, remains but below,
   Rememb'rance—tears—and the grave!

The last notes of the plaintive melody fell tremblingly from the singer's lips, nor was her grandfather less moved than she, as he tenderly placed a hand on her dark tresses, for in the blessing that he uttered, fell tears of sorrow, too.

"Was that a new song, my child?" asked the Rabbi Solomon, for such was his name. "I have never heard thee sing it before?"

"Nay, grandfather," answered the fair creature, a faint blush mantling her cheek, which was of the hue of ivory, "I composed it, even as I sang it, for the Spirit came over me."

"May the Spirit come over me, as well," said the old man, with strange earnestness, "so that I may save the righteous from the hand of the evil-doer."

Now let us leave the Rabbi and his granddaughter for awhile and learn the cause of their anxiety. In Moscow, where the Jews had then settled—after having been torn from their homes, their property destroyed, and their very privileges as human creatures laughed to scorn—lived an avaricious minister, who did all in his power to have them expelled from the country. In vain he looked for a reason to have them dismissed, he could find nothing against them; for they were peaceable, harmless, and the most industrious portion of the community. This Minister, Radamoff by name, was a great favourite with the Czar, who, though not so black-hearted as his servant, yet cordially disliked the Israelites on account of their being thrifty, hardworking and saving, whereas his subjects were lazy, and given to spending their all on Vodka. Besides, Czar as he was, he was not above wishing to replenish his impoverished coffers with the Jews' honest savings.

It so happened on the night Leah sang to her grandfather that it was the night before the eve of Passover; and, knowing this, Radamoff thought it a fitting time to work a plot he had planned against the Jews. On the night in question he feigned to be sad and downcast, as though a sudden misfortune had befallen him; so well indeed was his misery acted that the Czar was struck by it, and kindly asked the reason of his discomfiture.

"What aileth thee, Radamoff?" he asked of his favourite.

The conversation took place in an apartment

in the Imperial Palace, where the Emperor and his minister some times sat together discussing the affairs of state and other things which come not under the heading of politics.

"My Lord is too good and great," returned the other, "for him to heed the grief of one of his most miserable servants."

"Nay; I insist on knowing the cause of thy sorrow," cried the Czar, on whose weak heart the broken tones of his favourite had a visible effect. "And if it be in my power I will help thee."

"I mourn for my country—I mourn for the Christians," cried the wily Radamoff, as though the confession were wrung from him.

"How?" demanded the Monarch completely mystified, "doth aught threaten my subjects of which I know naught?"

"The Jews!—the Jews!" ejaculated Radamoff, falling on his knees before his Sovereign, as though in an agony of supplication. "He bites," he thought, as he watched between his fingers the rapid changes pass over the Czar's face.

"What is it with these Jews?" exclaimed he, wrathfully. "Am I destined never to hear the end of them? They are always doing some mischief which none can find out. I command thee to tell me instantly what new devilment they have perpetrated."

"The day after to-morrow is their Passover," rapidly answered Radamoff, "and to-morrow night a Christian will be slain to supply them with blood for their unholy rite."

The ruler rose from his seat and strode up and down the magnificent chamber in a great wrath.

"If this be true," he cried between his clenched teeth, showing them in all ferocity, as one of his own Siberian wolves might, "then I swear to Heaven that those who take part in the murder shall be flayed alive, and every other Jew driven out of the Empire."

This arrangement suited the avaricious Minister admirably, for many of the Israelites, reaping the reward of their indefatigable industry, had become exceedingly wealthy.

"Now," thought he, "I shall not only satisfy my hatred of them, but I shall be able to seize on most of their valuable possessions."

"Remember," observed the Czar, as his precious minister was leaving the apartment, "we must have proof positive of the Jews' guilt, otherwise the people will condemn thee if thou seek'st to slay the innocent."

Without having been told at the beginning of this tale, my reader will know I am writing of that which happened long ago, when even the Russian people were like the rest of humanity, and would not see a wrong done with impunity. To-day—ah! to-day—they have changed!

"Fear not, Sire," answered Radamoff, "their guilt shall be proved so indisputably that the people themselves shall wish to tear them in pieces."

And it came to pass that on the same night that this transpired in the Imperial Palace, the good old Rabbi Solomon, retiring to rest in his humble dwelling, had a wondrous vision. He thought he had fallen asleep, and this sleep might have lasted for two hours, when he was awakened by the sound of sweet music, the like of which he had never heard in all his days before. He sat up, entranced and bewildered; when lo and behold! it seemed as though the ceiling of his room was lifted up—up—up, he knew not whither, and, instead, his awestruck eyes rested on a dazzling throng of lovely forms, whom he knew to be angels. Then he saw them divide themselves into two groups—one to the right and one to the left—and in the centre appeared a long, long flight of steps, as though reaching from the blue empyrean, as white as alabaster, and shining like the sun, and down this flight of stairs he saw a figure descend, with looks of divine love and beatitude on his countenance. Nearer and nearer approached this glorious form, which was that of an old and a young man harmoniously blended together, until it stood at the last step, leaning on a staff that had the appearance of a sunbeam.

"Dost thou know me, my son?" asked the vision.

"Thou art Father Abraham," answered the Rabbi in Hebrew, with a blessing; "on whose bosom is life for evermore. Blessed art thou to eternity."

"Dost thou fear me?" said the vision, gently.

"Were my love less, oh Father, my fears would be great indeed. But I love thee," he added simply.

A smile of infinite loving-kindness overspread his face.

"Ask me what thou wilt," said the vision again.

"Nay; speak thou, thy son heareth," returned the Rabbi. "Oh! tell me why thou hast come to me, and not I to thee, seeing that I am not dead."

"Thy people are threatened with destruction, my son."

"Alas! I know it. How—how can I avert the calamity?"

"I will show thee," said the vision; and forthwith he made signs, and spoke in a tongue which the good Rabbi, learned as he was, could not understand.

However, he uttered a fervent and pious prayer, and soon after fell asleep, and was only awakened by the appearance of the warm morning sun peering into his room.

He told no one of his wonderful visitation, although he marvelled much to know the meaning of the strange words and signs which the vision of Abraham had uttered and made. About mid-day he was shocked and pained to find that many of his congregation had been grievously insulted by their Christian neighbours.

They complained to him how they had been hooted, chased, and even beaten in the public streets; and how they had been called "murderers," and that no official would interfere in their behalf. The Rabbi Solomon was at a loss to know from which quarter those cruel annoyances sprung, and sorrowed much that he had not been able to understand the signs of the vision of the night before. Towards eventide his granddaughter, Leah, who had been out walking with her old nurse, returned home with her great eyes humid with tears, and her raven tresses disordered with running.

"Oh, my grandfather!" she sobbed out. "God's people are indeed undone, for they now accuse us in the town of having stolen a Christian child, to use her blood for our Passover."

"God hath never deserted His beloved, nor will He now," murmured the Rabbi, softly. "Heed them not, my Leah, the hour of deliverance is at hand, when we shall weep no more."

What the young maiden had said was too true. Radamoff had ordered one of his servants to steal a Christian child, and his hirelings had bruited the story abroad that the Jews had stolen a child for her blood. The child's parents ran about the city with their story of woe, and demanded their little one. Already the foolish and cruel falsehood had found credence with the wisest and best citizens.

It was with a sad heart that the Rabbi on the Eve of Passover sought his bed, and long and fervently he prayed that he might be directed in what manner he might save his people from the danger that threatened them.

In the middle of the night, lo and behold he heard a voice which said to him :

"Art thou there, Solomon, my son ?"

And he answered after the manner of the Prophet of old :

"Speak, thou man of God, for His servant heareth."

And he opened his eyes, and the vision of Abraham, as on the preceding night, was before him. Then his heart leaped with a great joy, and he blessed God exceedingly.

Again he saw the long, long flight of stairs of dazzling whiteness, and once more he saw the form, as that of an old and young man harmoniously blended, leaning on the staff like a sunbeam. Myriads of beautiful forms thronged each side of the stairs, as though waiting on him.

"Yet a little while, and I shall be with you again," said the vision of Abraham to the Angels, and then the Rabbi Solomon saw the seraphs and the snow-white steps disappear, and the form of Abraham, shrouded in light, stood alone in the room.

"Thou didst not understand me yesternight, my son, and I forgot that the language spoken on high is not understood by mortals. See, I am come now to rectify my error."

"O, my God!" cried the Rabbi, whilst a great wave of joy spread over his heart, clearing his fears away. "How shall I extol thee, thou who hast lifted up my soul from the grave, so that thy servant and his flock go not down into the bottomless pit? Holy, holy, holy is Thy name, O! Lord of Hosts, and blessed art Thou for evermore."

The vision of Abraham looked upwards as the other spoke, as though to bless him silently.

"Come now, my son, and follow me," spoke Abraham, "and I will show thee what is to be done to baulk the designs of Israel's enemies."

Then, beckoning the Rabbi to follow him, the vision went from the room, and the Rabbi Solomon found he was leading him out of the house into the silent streets.

"Fear not," said the vision, as though he divined something that was passing in the other's mind. "None shall see thee, and thy grandchild is as safe in the house as though, indeed, she were amidst the Blessed. For she is guarded by angels."

A few yards from the Rabbi's dwelling stood the synagogue, which was a very large, albeit, unpretending structure.

Ungainly and poor though the building was, yet, I wot, God listened to the prayers of the worshippers in that humble place as much, aye, and more, than the orizons of those who thronged the magnificent Cathedrals in the fashionable quarters.

The Rabbi Solomon, felt not the cold, although his feet were bare and his body clad but in one thin garment. The watch passed him crying:

The clock has stricken three,
 But the City is free
From sin and harm.
 Then be ye calm,
  Good citizens.

The man's rough jacket touched the Rabbi, and the former trembled as though suddenly stricken with ague. But the man saw him not, because he walked with the servant of God.

The vision and the Rabbi entered the sacred building, and the former led his follower up to that part of the building where the ark stood. Now the ark is the repository of the tables of the covenant amongst the Jews. Here were also vessels which, according to custom, had been filled by the Rabbi.

"With what hast thou filled the vessels, my son?" asked the vision, mildly.

"With wine, oh, thou blessed servant of the Lord," answered the Priest, a little surprised at the question, "according to the law of the Israelites."

"See what they contain now!"

The Priest did as he was bidden, and a cry of

horror arose from his lips as in a hoarse voice he called out :

" It is blood ! human blood ! Oh, God !"

Although dark everywhere else, just where they stood fell a strong ray of light, more powerful even than the sun, which clearly showed to the Priest that it was indeed what he said, had any doubts arisen in his mind.

" All the vessels contain blood," spoke the vision sadly.

" Command me what to do with them," said the Rabbi tremblingly; "for the blood of a human being is too holy a thing that I should pour it away as water."

The angel looked at the old man, and his glance was so full of holy radiance and divine love that he was dazzled, and closed his eyes, and lo and behold ! when he opened them again the vessels stood in their accustomed places full of wine, nor was there a sign or trace of blood about them or anywhere else. The Rabbi questioned not as to how this miracle came about, but accepted what his Maker sent him with silent and devout gratitude.

" Who did this cruel thing, Father Abraham,

so that thy descendants and that of Isaac and Israel should die?" asked the Rabbi, at last, in tones, where reverence to that which he addressed, and anger of whom he spoke, were strongly mingled.

"The Czar's Minister, Radamoff. But return my son, it waxeth late, and I must away."

Then they left the Synagogue, and returned to the Rabbi's house in the same way as they had come from it. The good old man lay down on his bed, and as he saw the vision of Abraham fade away with the same look of divine love and beatitude as when he first saw it, he felt as though he would depart with him. He mourned that he should leave him, so much did his soul cleave to the servant of the Most High. However, he sunk into a deep slumber, and was only awakened by hearing a clamouring as of many voices in anger outside his house. He rose, and hastily throwing a white mantle, fashioned like a toga, round him, went to the casement to ascertain the meaning of the extraordinary occurrence. What was his astonishment to see the street crowded with people who seemed full of rage, judging by the terrible execrations that filled the air with unholy music.

Amidst that wild din of many blasphemous and angry tongues, he could hear that the populace accused him—him the God-fearing and loving, gentle priest—of murder! But a strange, holy calm pervaded his heart, even when he heard them threaten to raze his house to the ground, for he was armed without by possessing that ægis shield within—a quiet and good conscience.

"Open, in the Czar's name!" thundered one at the head of a body of soldiers.

The Rabbi hastened to his door, and, opening it, stood like a picture of some old Saint, with his snowy locks falling over his shoulders, and his white beard sweeping over the folds of his mantle.

He confronted Radamoff and —the Czar.

He made an obeisance, and mildly asked what they wished of him.

"Thou hast slain a Christian child for thy vile rites," boldly said Radamoff. "Come with us unto thy Tabernacle, for it is there where we shall find the blood of the unfortunate creature."

"Be it as you wish, but the Lord will judge between us," answered the Rabbi.

"Come with us now, wretch," cried Radamoff,

"and presume not to stand here parleying before the Czar."

They forced him to lead the way to the Synagogue, the crowds behind shouting maledictions on the priest's head, and threatening to tear him limb from limb. The guards, at a sign from the cruel minister, broke open the doors of the sacred edifice, at which insult the Rabbi's eyes flashed, and his blood surged within him as with the indignation of youth.

"Respect this place," he cried out, with a mighty voice, so all did hear him. "For it is not dedicated to a false God, or a graven image, but one Universal God—your God as well as our God. The Lord of Mercy, as he shall be the Lord of Wrath."

These words, spoken in sonorous tones, coupled with the majestic and dignified bearing of the old man, had great effect. The crowds thronged the place of worship in silence; whilst the Czar, Radamoff, and the guards who surrounded the former, walked towards the Ark, led by the Rabbi.

"Ay, 'tis here where you keep your vessels," said the relentless Radamoff, exultantly. "For

I have been a witness of your Jewish rites, before to-day. Bring forth the cups, and lay them at the feet of His Imperial Majesty the Czar."

The Czar stood a little way off partially surrounded by his guards with folded arms looking at the Jewish priest; for something, he knew not what, rivetted his eyes and attention on his person. Near him stood Radamoff, triumph glistening in his Tartar eyes, although his countenance was hypocritically mournful, as though he were shocked to be present at so horrible an occasion. Silence reigned as deep as Eternity, and the people who thronged the Synagogue seemed to have hushed their breaths.

The Rabbi, with an unsung hymn of praise and rejoicing in his heart, brought forth the vessels, and set them at the feet of the Czar, who, however, still remained as though transfixed, his eyes still resting on the Jew.

Then the sun burst forth and a great stream of light shone full upon the old priest's face, and his lips wore a smile of loving recollection, for had not yesternight the vision of Abraham trod in the very same spot where he, Solomon, now stood?

A murmur arose amidst the people, as though they whispered :

"Look, look, he is a man of God, although he be a Jew."

But he heard them not, for his thoughts were elsewhere, and it seemed as though the vision of Abraham had left a strange glory on his face, even as Moses had when he descended from Mount Sinai after he had communed with God.

"See ! see, Sire !" cried Radamoff, growing uneasy and anxious to have the affair at an end. "These vessels are full of blood."

"Nay, your sight misgives you," mildly spoke the Rabbi, suddenly called back by the voice of his cruel enemy. "They are full of wine."

"'Tis blood I say," cried Radamoff, fiercely, blinding himself to the fact. "If 'tis wine," he added, with a satanic laugh, "drink Jew."

"Right willingly, Christian," answered the Rabbi, and taking one of the cups at the Czar's feet, he quaffed from the vessel many times.

At this act the autocrat with an effort seized two of the vessels and examined them closely, After a little time he tasted of them.

"The Rabbi says truly," he observed, gravely,

yet with a slight ring of disappointment in his voice. " These vessels contain wine, and that of the best."

" 'Tis false, false, false !" almost shrieked Radamoff in a frenzy.

An angry frown gathered over the despot's brow.

" The Lord hath judged between thee and me," the old priest said, devoutly. " And His people are saved this day, as they were saved in years gone by from the devices of the wicked Haman. The blood these vessels once contained was of thy shedding. Christians! a Christian hath slain a child amongst you !"

" Who told thee ?" shrieked Radamoff, cowering before the priest.

" Abraham," solemnly answered the Israelite. " He descended even from Heaven to warn me."

The Minister, had, indeed, committed the horrid crime of slaying the child stolen by one of his servants, and putting her blood into the vessels, so that the Jews should be annihilated.

At this answer a terrible yell burst from the throat of the wretched Minister, and he fell prone to the ground in a pool of blood. When they went to raise him, according to the Czar's command, their warm, living hands touched a cold, lifeless corpse.

"Oh, God!" prayed the Jewish priest over his fallen Christian foe, "show compassion to the wicked. They need thy mercy most who have sinned most. The good have already been blessed by Thee in being good."

Then the people, recognising the hand of God in the awful punishment that befel the Minister, knelt down—they that had come to slay—and worshipped with the priest of Israel in his place of worship. For in great calamities, or in great triumphs, especially those concerning the mind, men must fly to that which is infinite.

Seek not for this brief story in the hope to find it recorded in the annals of history; and seek for it not in the worm-eaten chronicles of the scribe, for it was but written in the hearts of men at the time it happened; and when these hearts became dust it was forgotten, like all that is good and noble too often is.

But of this thing I am certain. When the Day of Reckoning comes, when nations shall be gathered together, and barbaric rulers weighed in the balance with the poorest beggar; then, for each groan of anguish wrung from the hearts of an unoffending and industrious race, a just and merciful God shall claim indemnity a thousand-fold.

VERITAS.

Oh, Virtue! I have followed you through life and find you but a Shade.
Euripides.

Oh, Earth! all bathed with blood and tears; yet never Hast thou ceased putting forth thy fruit and flowers!
Corinne (Mme. de Stael) Translated.

VERITAS.

Mavorel was a writer. He was one of those kindly natured people who are always performing better acts for humanity than humanity does for them. In a word, he was a handsome and generous fellow, and one also at times impecunious. When he made an extra amount of money he would spend it royally in one night, in the company of one or more convivial friends. With gold in his pocket, nothing but the finest dinner, flanked by the finest wine, would suit him. The next day, in all probability, he would not have sufficient wherewith to buy a meal. However, this did not matter much, as his numerous friends idolised him, and willingly would have shared with him the proverbial crust, although, possibly, they would not have been quite so generous with their purses. Of course, Mavorel had his light-o'-loves—for what man, whether writer or otherwise, hath not—but even in these his nobler feelings asserted themselves and no word of love ever escaped him to delude earth's most unfortunate creatures. He respected innocence, and no young girl had ever been tempted from the path of virtue by him. He argued within himself that there was plenty of sin in the world and that he had no desire to add to it.

One night he found himself landed high and dry in his modest lodgings with a very vacant feeling in his stomach, and only a modest silver coin to satisfy it in his pocket. There was no food in the house and nothing ordered, and he found after deep cogitation that he would have to seek a meal out of doors. He thought, with his mouth watering, how famously he had supped the night before on hare soup, on soles cooked in white wine, on grilled crab, on roast partridges with cream sauce and oysters stewed in champagne, and he cursed himself for not having had a less Lucullus-like feast, so he should have had at least a sovereign in his pocket to-night. But he was always doing the same thing, and all his resolutions to save came to nothing. Besides, if he only dined sumptuously himself it would not be so bad; it would not make such a big hole in his pocket. But he had no appetite to dine alone. He must bring one or more friends with him. That was what emptied this good-for-nothing's pocket. This good-for-nothing, for whom even the crustiest and most austere of beings had a good word to say. Mavorel, full of hunger and philosophy—for it is curious how hunger will make some men philosophical—put on his hat and coat, and was soon one amidst the hurrying pedestrians in the street.

"Now what shall I do?" he thought. "Shall I get a dish of meat, bread, potatoes with my money or—what now?"

This last ejaculation was caused by the fact of an old pedlar falling heavily against him, pushed by a thoughtless member of the moving throng.

"How now?" exclaimed Mavorel again, "What's the matter, old man?"

The man addressed seemed in a sort of stupor, and, seeing this, the writer hastily dragged him into a side street, for the sight of the cadaverous face, with the long, white beard, tattered garments, and sunken eyes of the old man touched his compassionate heart.

"I am starving!" faltered the old man, opening his eyes, and straightening himself with an effort, "I have not eaten a crust of bread since the day before yesterday, and I cannot sell my wares."

"Here, my poor friend; your wants are greater than mine," said Mavorel, unconsciously adopting a great and gentle courtier's famous speech, and casting his last piece of silver hastily in the trembling hand of the beggar, he left him, and was soon lost in the street again, which was like a restless ocean with human waves.

Mavorel remembered suddenly that he had an important article to write, and, finding he would have no more time to wander about or to seek his friends, returned home, and, filling his pipe, smoked placidly for a few moments. Finding this conducive to writing, he sat himself down to work in earnest. Scarcely had he been seated for a few moments than he heard a knock at his door, which he followed up by a cheery invitation for his visitor to enter.

The door opened, and, before he was aware, the old pedlar whom he had assisted in the street, stood before him.

"Old man, you walk quickly," exclaimed

Mavorel, not best pleased to find who his visitor was.

"Are you ashamed of your charity?" asked the visitor. "Am I not flesh and blood like yourself? Do you think that money is all a beggar wants? Have they no human feelings like yourself? Do you think that the heart of the beggar yearns only for earthly food? Young man, I tell you that you know not humanity!"

"How so?" asked Mavorel, intensely surprised to hear the pedlar talk in this fashion.

"How so?" reiterated the stranger, "I shall tell you. After you helped me with your money you treat me with scorn because of my tattered garments. This shows your want, not of heart, but of knowledge of humankind. Do you think because my coat is torn and soiled that my soul cannot be immortal and clean? Are you better than a beggar? You who have to bow to earn your bread before men who are more foolish than you? Is a politician better than a beggar who cringes before a monarch for a place and sinecure? Is a king better than a beggar, when he is forced to pray God that his life may not be undone by a traitor's hand, and his throne unshaken by sedition? All men are beggars, and God the only Benefactor."

Mavorel recoiled from the old man half in fear, half in astonishment.

"You speak truly, old man," he observed at last, pensively.

"I do—hey?" chuckled the beggar, "for in truth, if I speak not truly, none can. But begging is after all but a sorry business. Last night as I was traversing a fashionable quarter I stopped in front of a fine mansion. Presently the portals of this mansion opened, and a young man with a frank face came out, and a handsome woman, with a shawl thrown over her head, kissed her hand to him from the window. 'I shall be back soon,' he said fondly. He was her husband. 'I shall count the hours, love, till you return,' she called back. The gates were closed, and he passed me and gave me a coin. He had scarcely turned the corner of the street when a carriage swiftly and silently came from another direction. A handsome and sinister man descended at the gates of the mansion, and opened them with a key of his own. Three hours afterwards he left the mansion, laughing. It was the old, old tale of the false friend, the false wife, and the unsuspicious and loving husband. The wicked man in passing me threw me a gold piece. Oh, how it weighs me down to accept the wages of the unrighteous; begging is indeed a sorry business."

"But who are you?" asked Mavorel. "You who are attired as a beggar, and talk like a philosopher."

"I am a magician," returned the old fellow. his eyes twinkling with a strange light.

"Some travelling charlatan," observed the writer, shrugging his shoulders. "I have met many of them before."

"You do not believe me then, when I tell you. that I am a real enchanter?"

"Certainly not!" answered Mavorel, as contemptuously as possible. "Do you take me for a dolt?"

The old beggar did not respond to his younger companion's scornful interrogatory, but laughed softly to himself.

"Thou art by no means a good host, my son," said the old man, "and since thou wilt not offer it I will help myself to thy excellent wine."

"In truth I have nothing," exclaimed Mavorel, ruefully.

"But I tell thee that thou hast," returned the stranger; and stepping to the sideboard he opened the cupboard thereof, and from thence sure enough drew two bottles which appeared full of wine.

"Here, drink!" he continued, pouring out a huge bumper for the young man. "It is the finest stuff that mortal ever tasted. The grapes from which it is made come from a portion of the vine grown in the Garden of Eden before man's fall."

The writer laughed incredulously, and took up the bumper. How the wine, yellow as gold, danced and foamed in the glass. It seemed as though fairy-like forms flitted upwards with the thousand bubbles that rose and broke on the surface.

"I drink to thy health, most noble magician!" Mavorel said, and tossed off the wine with a half mocking smile. "By the Gods, it is famous," he added, as he set down the glass, empty.

"Greybeard, give me more, whether 'tis grown in Hell or Heaven, it matters not. Thy wine is most excellent."

Chuckling quietly, the old man filled the writer's glass again, and yet again; until, indeed no more remained in the bottles. "Would'st thou have more; art thou hungry?" asked the stranger.

"I neither hunger or thirst for meat or drink; though I thirst indeed to know who you are?" cried the writer. The wine surged into his young blood, and heated him. "Tell me indeed who thou art, old quack!" he laughed boisterously, and seized him by the hand.

"Know then, I am that spirit which men call 'Truth,'" responded the stranger, in deep and sonorous tones, freeing himself from the young man's now awe-stricken clasp. "I have wandered over the earth for thousands of years. Young and beautiful I dwelt in the Garden of Eden ere Adam and Eve lied to Heaven's mighty King. Then I grew suddenly old, and thus wander ever. Men have eternally outraged my mandates, thus it is that I have clad myself in these tattered garments, for when the soul is in mourning, gay clothes are cast aside. Since men are liars, Truth must a beggar be; and I beg eternally for truth. Yes, I am the spirit called Veritas!"

Mavorel bent humbly before the Spirit, and said in a low, sad voice—

"I too have outraged thee, Veritas; pardon me, oh, pardon me!"

"Away with fear," answered Veritas, "you shall be my pupil, and I will teach thee some lessons; and show thee marvellous things."

Encouraged by the wine as much as by the reassuring words of the Spirit, Mavorel sprang to his feet, full of life and energy. Instead, however, of seeing before him a decrepit beggar, he beheld a handsome old man, of majestic aspect, wrapped in a mantle of some strange material, the texture of which mortal eye never beheld before.

"Come with me to my house," spake Veritas. "It is so narrow here."

They left Mavorel's lodgings then, and descended into the street. They walked together some distance, and at last approached a magnificent mansion, which Mavorel did not remember having seen before, although he was thoroughly acquainted with all parts of the city.

Veritas stopped before the gates of the mansion, and drawing forth a key, inserted it in the lock, which opened instantly. They entered, and the gates closed voluntarily behind them. The spirit Veritas led the way into the house, and passing some spacious corridors and ascending a marble staircase, the balustrades of which were of gold, inlaid with precious stones, at last opened the door of a chamber, into which he invited Mavorel to enter. Mavorel did so, and was astonished at the magnificence of which even the wildest dream of an Eastern, under the influence of hashish, could not picture forth. Overcome with wonder and excitement the young man sank in a divan, and exclaimed : " If this unparalleled splendour is the reward of Truth and Virtue, then I henceforth shall evermore be their disciple."

" Virtue and goodness lie but in the hearts of men," said Veritas. " They are least virtuous who strive to appear so. The followers of Truth often starve, and vice walks abroad in broadcloth. But what then ? Is virtue only to be practised like a craft ? "

"I swear by Heaven, I shall be thy apostle evermore, Veritas!" the young man cried ardently.

"Alas, stripling!" the Spirit spake mournfully. "I know too well the sons of man."

"But I am different. In good truth I am!" Mavorel said, quickly and warmly. "I am different to others! I can be noble and virtuous if I chose."

Veritas answered not, but sat beside the writer as though wrapped in deep meditation. Ever and anon he glanced at Mavorel, as though in pity, and then his eyes would lose that sorrowful look, and appear lost in speculation, of which Mavorel knew the world had no part. "But come!" he said abruptly, after a long pause, in which Mavorel examined the marvellous apartment, and each second bringing a fresh beauty to sight. "I have promised to show you some things, and I must perform what I have declared to you I would."

With these words Veritas raised his right hand, in which he held a short golden wand, and lo and behold! Mavorel perceived, at a little distance, a curtain as though made of crystal, flashing with jewels, and stretching from the lofty ceiling to the floor. Presently the curtain was drawn aside by an invisible agency, and he saw stretched before him another great and noble apartment in which was a throne, and on this throne sat a monarch. Round about him were courtiers and sycophants, lords of high degree and prelates the least amidst them. And all seemed well with the king, and his throne on a firm basis. But suddenly it appeared as though a veil fell from Mavorel's eyes. He saw that the King, though to all outward appearance magnanimous and splendid, was a poltroon and coward, and that the sword of Damocles hung over his head suspended by a hair.

"Why doth the potentate fear and tremble?" asked Mavorel.

"Because he uses his power to crush an industrious race; and he feels that the hour of retribution is always nigh. The wicked, however powerful, walk in dread, nor is that dread without foundation."

"I pray thee, Veritas, show me another scene, for in truth I meddle not with the fate of kings or countries," observed the writer, smiling, as the scene faded away, and the jewelled crystal curtain fell once more.

"So, ho!" laughed the Spirit, softly. "Be it as you wish," and again he raised his wand, and once more the crystal curtain was drawn aside.

This time, the scene which presented itself troubled Mavorel sorely. For stretched before him was a marvellous garden of flowers and shrubs, growing in rich profusion. There were fountains whose perfumed waters spouted up high, and fell sprinkling the jasmine, the roses, and magnolias. There was a stream whose waters were like molten gold rippling over pebbles of marble, on whose surface water-lilies lightly rested. The nightingales had already commenced their song, for the night had come, and the stars bedecked Heaven's blue canopy. In the midst of this beautiful garden—and it was this that troubled Mavorel greatly—was a bank of rare exotics; flowers whose faces were like human beings, some sad, some joyous, and some pensive, and seated on this bank was a personage of such dazzling beauty, the like of whom Mavorel had never dreamed of in his wildest dreams. A robe of samite was twisted about her in serpentine coils, and each coil seemed to have another colour. Her face, although beautiful in the extreme, wore a discontented expression, and her fair white hands were clasped nervously together. She wore but one jewel, and that was a diamond cross, the stones of which were so large and brilliant that it made the young man's eyes close involuntarily.

His breath came short and quickly. He wanted to rush forward, and throw himself at her feet, and beg a flower from her hand.

A strong grasp held him back.

"What are you doing?" asked Veritas, sternly. "Stay here."

The beautiful woman here rose from the bank of flowers, and stretched forth her arms imploringly to Mavorel.

"Take me, oh, take me!" she cried in a beseeching voice.

The young man rose again, and was again held back by Veritas.

"Let me go," he cried, in a choking voice.

"Stay! I command thee!"

"Take, oh, take me with thee," the woman cried again, in a voice of stronger entreaty.

"Dost hear me, greybeard? Let go, I say!" exclaimed the young man, overcome by the beauty of the woman, and forgetting who Veritas was.

"Thou shalt remain here," the Spirit said calmly.

"Take me, oh, take me!" the woman said again, coming forward and upsetting what little reason still remained in Mavorel's brain.

"This diamond cross will buy all we want. Let us fly from here."

"Mavorel, stay!" Veritas said, holding him back.

"Take me!" the woman cried again.

Seeing the old man would not free him from his powerful grasp, Mavorel seized a poniard, which, curiously enough, lay in close proximity, and, without another thought, plunged it into the old man's heart. He, with a groan of anguish, fell to the ground, dead!

Scarcely had Mavorel done this terrible deed than the whole air seemed to resound with cries of "Take me, take me!" until the place spun round him.

"Now come with me," the young man said in a

voice he scarce recognised as his own. " We will fly from here together."

The beautiful creature, for whom he had committed the fell act, advanced, and they both sought to find an exit from the room. But they looked in vain. The crystal curtain had fallen, closing the garden from view, so they could not search there.

Presently, as Mavorel walked hurriedly about, his foot struck the lifeless corpse of Veritas. Now he looked like the old beggar to whom he had given alms in the street, and then, his heat and passion being over, Mavorel felt his heart overcome with pity and remorse. He looked at the beautiful woman, and shuddered, wondering how his hand could have stricken down the gentle Spirit for her sake.

Tears of grief fell from his eyes, as he leant over the corpse, and, with a sudden desperate resolve, he plucked the poniard from Veritas" heart, and was just about to plunge it into his own, when his hand was stayed by a stronger one than his, and a known voice said:

"Thou see'st, Mavorel, it is not so easy to be virtuous."

The young writer turned, and beheld Veritas standing before him, majestic and benign as heretofore.

Mavorel fell on his knees to the Spirit, crying:

"Judge me as thou wilt. However severe the punishment, it cannot be as great as my crime!"

"Arise, poor youth!" Veritas spake compassionately. "Thy heart is good although thy principles are not strong. For yonder woman, who hath but outward beauty and no inward grace, thou wouldst have slain me; and so stained for ever thy immortal soul."

"Pardon me!" murmured Mavorel sorrowfully.

"I have pardoned thee. Go from here, and take with thee that creature for whom thou hadst committed a crime."

"I pray thee, most gentle Veritas!" the young man said falteringly. "Grant me yet another request ere I leave thee to spend in penance the rest of my days."

"Name thy wish," Veritas returned gently.

"That she whose face and words erst tempted me to sin may never come again before mine eyes," Mavorel answered, in a low tone, with his eyes bent and his arms folded across his breast.

"We love not then the companions of sin when sin has left us?" the Spirit said with half-jesting, half-kindly voice. "So be it then."

And lo, when the young man raised his eyes the beautiful woman had vanished, and he and Veritas stood alone in the room.

"Come Mavorel; ponder no more over thy sin. 'Twas but the fleeting poison of thy youth's young blood; and I have pardoned thee," Veritas said pityingly, touching the young man's hand.

"Would that I could forgive myself, as thou dost me!" answered Mavorel, "and that the memory of my deed need never come before me."

"Nay!" the Spirit made answer. "Even God is deprived of making that which is past never to have been. But thou shalt not leave me yet. I have more marvels still to show thee."

So saying, the spirit left Mavorel alone for a little while, and, when he returned, brought with him three urns of curious and fantastic workmanship. These he set down before the young writer, and bade him look at the inscription on each of them. Mavorel perceived some strange hieroglyphics carved on the lids, which he could not decipher, and Veritas said, mournfully shaking his head:

"Well do I believe, Oh! Son of Man, that canst not read these strange characters. Know, then, that the words inscribed on these vases, are in the language the world spoke ere the Tower of Babel was built. It was the only thing our first parents carried with them from Eden; and it was lost for evermore in Shinar, through the presumption of man, when he tried to build a tower reaching Heaven's Kingdom. On this one," he continued, pointing to the first urn, "is inscribed a word which meaneth 'Wisdom;' on the second is inscribed another word, which meaneth 'Virtue,' and on the third is written the word meaning 'Wealth.' Mavorel! I bid thee now to choose of the three, of which one thou wouldst wish to be possessed. Reflect, and speak, and I will grant it thee! What is thy desire? Wisdom, Virtue, or Wealth!"

The young man for a few moments was too overcome even to think. The prospect of an abundance of either Wisdom or Wealth dazzled his senses. But, on a sudden he became calm, and he spoke as in a soliloquy:

"If I were wealthy? Could wealth give me happiness? I have seen the rich miserable, because they have not wisdom; and I have seen the wise miserable, because they are not rich. A rich man hath no real friends, and I, a poor one, have. I am richer than the rich man. Shall I buy hypocrisy and flattery? If I am rich to-day, to-morrow my mind will cry for that which money cannot buy; therefore, Wealth, I'll none of thee. And, what sayest thou, oh! Wisdom? Thou, the only thing that can be taken with us beyond the grave? If I choose thee, the world will be mine own; kings will be my courtiers, and the universe my court. Wisdom can purchase riches, and I shall be rich, as well as wise. But stay! With Wisdom cometh discontent. For, when we are wise, all we know is, how little we know. And then Wisdom destroys love. For to love and be wise is denied even the Gods! Why should I, to obtain fame and power, renounce the dear friends of my youth? Those friends, who even now, as I stand here in this mystic place, come before me with their endless deeds of kindness; their tender laughter, and their songs. Wisdom would place me in a sphere beyond them, and never more could I be contented in their loved society. Shall I exchange Love for Wisdom? Love is the life of man, 'tis better than Fame, Power or Wisdom, therefore Wisdom," the young man continued, huge beads of perspiration dropping from his brow, and a sigh, deep and unutterable, breaking from his overcharged breast, "I renounce thee, and choose for myself, and all the world, Virtue."

He fell on his knees before the Spirit, tears flowing his eyes, and Veritas gazed at him with deeper compassion and kindliness yet.

"I pray thee, Spirit of Truth and Love!" Mavorel said imploringly, raising his tearful eyes to Veritas, "not only implant Virtue in my heart, but in that of every heart of the whole Universe. Hypocrisy and Falsehood have reigned too long. Grant, oh! Veritas, thy gentle sway, and Virtue now should reign instead."

"Thy wish, poor dreaming youth, shall be granted," the Spirit made answer, mournfully.

"Now come with me, we must away, and see the effect of Virtue's sway."

The writer, Mavorel, rose, at the behest of Veritas, and, following in his footsteps, left the place in the same way as they had entered it. Once out in the street, Veritas stretched out his arms, and murmured an incantation, no word of which the young man understood. The evening sky was studded with thousands of twinkling stars, yet, when the Spirit spoke, it seemed as though they came nearer earth to listen. It was a strange and preternatural hush, followed suddenly by hideous screeching, and other horrible sounds.

Horror-stricken, Mavorel asked to know whence these terrible noises emanated.

"They come from the Spirits that prompt murder, theft, lying, treachery, and rapine," answered Veritas. "They are flying to Hell, for Virtue hath begun to rule the world, and they must leave it."

They walked on, seeing all, but invisible. Presently they came across a man, stealing along in the shadows with a sack on his shoulders.

"That man is bent on mischief," Mavorel said. "Do not permit him to accomplish his work, dear Veritas."

"Peace, my son," Veritas spake benevolently, "in that sack he carries stolen goods, which he intends returning to their rightful owner."

After walking on for a while longer, Mavorel observed, that from a house where noisy characters usually assembled for dancing and drinking, all was still and silent.

"Where are the inmates of yonder house," he asked, wonderingly.

"Gone to pray for their past sins," Veritas answered, quietly.

Then, wandering on still further, they came across a well-known place where Mavorel and his friends assembled to make night merry with their laughter and their songs. They found it without light, and silent as the grave.

"Where are the friends of my heart?" cried Mavorel, fearfully, "where are the sounds which gladdened my ears? Where are the forms that gladdened my sight? Are they all dead, or whither have they gone? Tell me, tell me, Veritas."

"They have gone for ever!" the Spirit answered. "To those of many sins, Death hath come in a terrible shape, for Virtue hath come to them, and they have taken their own lives ; and to those of lesser sins, they, ah ! they have gone into a hermitage or sought a nunnery."

And they wandered on, Mavorel now filled with grief at the loss of his friends.

"Am I better than they ? " he mused, "that I should not share their fate. Better that I were dead with those with whom I sinned and loved than living and virtuous with those whom I love not ! "

Presently they came to a house at whose door Mavorel saw a woman weeping bitterly.

"What aileth her ? " he asked.

"See yonder," Veritas made answer, "there is a man. They intended to fly together, but the voice of conscience whispered 'Virtue' and she cannot go ! "

Mavorel observed a man in the road leaning against a post, with his face buried in his handkerchief.

"Who is he ? " he asked.

" Her lover ! " returned the Spirit.

"And who is that man praying by his bedside ?" demanded the young man again.

" That is her husband."

They continued their walk, and together they went into the palace of a King. They saw him surrounded by courtiers on a throne, and presently a dignitary, in ermine and purple robes, came forward, and said:

"Sign this, Sire; for doing to death a virtuous man, a villain is condemned to die; this is the document which will seal his doom. The world will be well rid of the monster."

The King turned pale and trembled.

"Oh God!" he cried out in a mighty voice. "If I sign the death-warrant of a man who hath caused the death of but one person, what infernal doom shouldst thou not mete out to me, who have done away with a thousand noble men?"

And with his hands to his face, the King left the throne-room, and the document was left unsigned.

Veritas left the palace with the awe-stricken and sorrowful Mavorel, and walked on with him until he came to the strand of a mighty sea.

The tide was going out, and the waters made a weird sort of music together, accompanied by the clashing of the myriads of little stones. Calm, and holy, unlike the once vice perturbed world the moon shone down serenely on all, but most on the face and form of a drowned young girl. The face was beautiful in death, and the lank, long, golden hair served only as a frame to the sweet lifeless portrait of her spirit. Mavorel shuddered with horror as he saw the poor creature.

" Why tremblest thou, my son?" asked Veritas. "Death to this poor creature came as comfort, not as terror. Pity those who die yellow and sered in sin, and not those green and young to it."

" But my father," cried Mavorel, brokenly, " why should death steal this fair and lovely flower, are there no sapless trees for him to take instead ?"

" She loved, and sinned," Veritas answered, "and she knew that death alone could wash that sin away from her stain'd soul. But come away. The watchmen are wending their way hither to take the poor inanimate thing away."

"Unhappy soul, that erstwhile lived in that beautiful cage," Mavorel exclaimed, brokenly, apostrophising the dead girl. " Wing thy way to Heaven, and in thy prayers for all mankind, remember the pity of one poor sinner too."

Scarcely had they left the spot, where already some men had lifted up the body of the girl, when they came across a young man standing on a rock, not far distant. The youth's eyes were dry and tearless, though an unnatural pallor was spread over his countenance. Mavorel felt himself curiously drawn towards him.

"Who is that young man," he asked gently, "tell me, thou who art even more than my father?"

"Away, away, from this spot!" exclaimed Veritas, in a terror-stricken voice. "And weep, Mavorel, that thou belong'st to the unhappy race of man."

"But father, who, who is this sad-faced youth?"

"Draw nearer then, Mavorel, look at that pallid cheek. Once it was coloured with a hue of rose equal to thine own. Look at his emaciated form, his trembling step, his feeble hands; yet time was, when all were robust and firm, with a soul to dare and an arm to strike against tyranny and wrong. Look into that eye where all spirit and fire is lost, and life too, but that remorse holds its own with fiend-like energy. That man loved that dead girl, and in a moment of forgetfulness they sinned against the laws of Heaven. Alas! that sin is so short; and remorse so long. Those ears, opened but to hear the voice of pure love and virtue, gave themselves up to listen to levity. Levity is an easy step to inconstancy, and inconstancy to falsehood. Those eyes that shrank from the sight of wrong, now sought to find it, and the heart once free from worldliness and vice, sought both unconsciously. That tongue, once the herald of honesty and affection, became hypocritical and lying. It betrayed his first love, and it betrayed his friend. For a sin that he himself was guilty of, he allowed another to suffer, and then came the terrible night; the terrible night, Mavorel, when I accorded thee thy wish, my son, that humanity should become virtuous. Behold that unfortunate youth, in a few minutes he will have sought the waters as his grave, for his remorse brings him hither to drown himself!"

"Hold him back, Veritas!" cried Mavorel, his heart nigh bursting with grief. "With all those sins on his soul, a man dare not appear before his Maker."

"My son!" spake the Spirit, "my power endeth here. He hath perpetrated the crimes, and he must expiate them. He is but doing that which is virtuous and right."

"Oh, Father, oh, Father of Truth!" cried the young man, throwing himself at his feet, his eyes overflowing with tears. "Be again to mankind as thou wast when I first met thee, a beggar amongst them. Give them back their burden of crime, and take away their gnawing sense of guilt. Give mankind their iniquities again, and take away this cruel remorse. Give—give to man his sins again!"

Mavorel, the writer, awoke! Sin reigned supreme.

HOW TOM BELLAMY WON MY LORD HERTFORD'S WAGER.

No friend's a friend till he shall prove himself a friend.
Beaumont and Fletcher.

Some friendships are made by Nature; some by contract; some by interest; and some by souls.
Jeremy Taylor.

HOW TOM BELLAMY WON MY LORD HERTFORD'S WAGER,

(WRITTEN BY HIMSELF IN FORM OF A LETTER TO A FRIEND, JUNE 18TH, 1762.)

London.

MY DEAR HARRY,

In acceding to thy earnest wish, that I should relate to thee in full that episode which is now the talk of the town—and White's—I feel if I am giving thee that satisfaction I am also guilty of discomfiting thee, for I must either tell thee the incident at length, or not at all. But never shall it be said that I, Thomas Bellamy, turned a deaf ear to a friend's demand, no matter how slight.

Know then in the first instance, that after I left college, I ran wild about town for a year or so, then finding the life suited neither my purse nor my health, accepted the post of Secretary to my Lord Hertford, whom thou knowest as well as I and the world do. I consider him one of the ablest men in this country, one of the handsomest, and one of the most dissolute to boot, yet withal possessing the finest heart in the world. Nature has spoiled him, and he, not to be behindhand, hath spoiled Nature. Gambling, drink, and debauch are ruining him, yet could my hand and soul reform him, they would be sacrificed to save him. Well, to my story; as I know thou hadst never a mind for platitudes. It happened in this way, my Lord and I set out on a journey to Norfolk, whither he had been invited by a kinswoman, who owns one of the finest estates in the county. It chanced that when the coach had proceeded about a quarter of the journey a wheel came off; and lo, and behold we were in a sorry predicament. However, as luck would have it, we were near an inn, and some of the attendants, seeing the mishap, rushed out to assist us, then we sought shelter until such a time when the coach should be restored to its former condition. We were shown into an old-fashioned room, the lattices of which were thrown wide open, and the flower-laden, balmy air poured in, replacing with a sweeter fragrance the sweet Virginian tobacco we smoked. For no sooner did the accident happen than my lord lighted his pipe, and I did so too. Where women fly to tears and hysterics, men seek the more magic and more soothing power of tobacco. Cleopatra would never have exercised—no, nor Helen of Troy, either—such a sway over the hearts of men had tobacco existed in those days. Tobacco divides that affection in the masculine heart which was once woman's alone. Well, we were scarce seated five minutes when, with the blossom and grass perfumed air floated in the sound of human voices in angry discussion, and one, louder than the rest, execrating in a most godless fashion.

" By G——, I'll shoot that horse," cried the voice, outside.

" But master," answered what seemed a groom, " it isn't Diana's fault, she's dead tired, that's what she is, master. The other 'osses have been changed twice, and she not at all !"

"Hold your —— tongue!" cries out the first voice, peremptorily. " Go and have this nag put up. I wonder what sort of accommodation they can afford a man in this cursed out-of-the-way hole. Look you, if Diana doesn't behave in better fashion to-morrow, I'll let daylight into her, by G——, I will!"

There was a clank of spurred boots along the stones, and then the horses clattered off, and the voices in the courtyard ceased.

"I know that voice," presently said my lord, breaking silence. "It belongs to Calvert Cresswell, for a hundred guineas!"

I recognised the gentleman's mode of speaking, not his voice. There's not another man about town who swears so extravagantly as Calvert Cresswell doth. Thou knowest him, Harry, well enough. He's a tall, handsome, dark-complexioned fellow, with a swaggering air, and black eyes with a touch of hell fire in them. He is a pretty frequent visitor at my lord's house, and seems a favourite, too, in a way. But there's something about the man I thoroughly mistrust, and I was right, as thou wilt presently see.

I agreed with my lord that it was Calvert Cresswell, and off he darted to bring him into the parlour, telling me not to go away in the meantime. I was not left alone long for the door was opened, and my lord re-entered, followed by his friend. He greeted me in a manner which showed me that he far preferred my room to my company; as for me I smiled as blandly and amiably as possible, feeling I should like to meet him behind Montague House, with a couple of friends and a brace of pistols. After we had partaken of some cold viands, he became communicative and rattled off some lively stories, all of which he was the hero, and various lovely females the heroines and—victims.

"By the way, whither are you bound?" asked my lord, breaking in somewhat impatiently on a particularly aggravating *conte d'amour*.

"To the very place where you are!" answers Mr. Cresswell. "I am going on a visit to your kinswoman, Lady Francis Ravenscroft."

"Are you going there?" asks my lord, raising his finely pencilled eyebrows.

"Yes; why not?" says the other, shrugging his shoulders. "You have the monopoly of most things, my lord, but not all."

"Methought," observes my patron, coolly, but gravely, "That Othello was jealous of Desdemona."

"My lord," answers Calvert Cresswell, cynically, "if we were all to heed the idle jealousies of husbands of handsome women, some of us would have to stay at home all our days, I warrant."

There was a pointedness about this worldly remark which was not lost upon Lord Hertford. He smiled, shrugged his shoulders in his turn, and suggested, with a yawn, that they should have a game of cards.

I knew it would not be long ere they betted on something; it seems as natural to the world of fashion as life itself. I couldn't help laughing though when, as quick as thought, both gentlemen drew from their pockets a pack of cards, simultaneously.

Mr. Cresswell's pack was chosen as it was the cleaner, and my lord shuffled.

"What shall we play for?" he asked.

"My soul!" says Cresswell, laughingly, cutting the pack.

"Nay," replies the other, dealing, "your soul's already won."

"Ay," retorted his friend, "by the very one who hath yours. And," he added sarcastically, "could it be in better keeping than with him who has charge of one so eminent as is my lord's of Hertford? By the way, the last time we played together it was for a woman."

Do you remember the talk, Harry, how Lord Hertford and Mr. Calvert Cresswell played for Cresswell's notorious but beautiful mistress, Nellie Flouncewell? You'll remember, too, that my lord won, and Mistress Nellie turned out to be a spy, besides a courtesan.

"Yes, and a d———d bad one!" assented my patron.

"Come, now," asks Mr. Cresswell sneeringly. "Surely you didn't expect to play for a good one, Oh, fie!"

"Yes, and I have to thank young Bellamy for finding out what a thoroughly dangerous female pretty Nellie was," remarked my lord, coldly.

He alluded to some treasonable papers I had found by the merest accident in his mistress's possession, and which was the cause of her dismissal.

"Oho!" exclaims Cresswell, laying his cards down, and fixing his insolent black eyes on me; yet withal with a certain sort of interest.

"Rather a young sort of champion, is'nt he?"

"Youth has nothing to do with it, sir," I responded, somewhat hotly. "And surely a young friend is better than an old traitor."

Calvert Cresswell scowled. "Faith, do you imagine you can defend my lord against all his antagonists?" he asked.

"Nay, only some of them," I returned, gravely and meaningly.

"Poor enemies!" he ejaculated, scornfully. "But I suppose my lord can defend himself against his foes without your help."

"Every man can guard against an open foe, but few against secret ones," I replied, laconically.

"Hear, hear!" cries out my lord, puffing out huge volumes of smoke, and Calvert Cresswell slightly blushed at my plain speaking.

He affected to be amused with me, and laughed, but there was something unreal about it, that showed me he was not quite at his ease regarding me. However, as he picked up his cards, everything was soon forgotten in the excitement of the game. Higher and higher rose the stakes until even I stood aghast at the sums these two gentlemen lost and won.

"Curse it! You've the devil's luck!" cries out Cresswell, at last throwing down his cards. "Every card is against me, I won't play any more to-night. I don't mind losing, but can't stand against infernal luck as yours. But I'll tell you what it is," he exclaimed, suddenly, as though struck with a bright idea. "Let's bet!"

"Right willingly," quoth my lord, with that lazy good humour common to a man who is used to victory. "But I warn you before hand that you'll lose."

"H'm, yes! men always do against you; your luck is proverbial."

"What's the bet you propose?" questioned my Lord Hertford.

"Simply this. Let us both start off on our journey to-morrow by two different routes, and the one who reaches the Castle first shall be paid by the one who arrives after him the sum of ten thousand guineas. I'll bet ten thousand; curse me!—fifteen thousand—to your ten!"

"Nay, as for that," puts in my lord, "we'll have an even wager."

" Done ! So be 't, then !" answers the other.

" I accept the bet with pleasure, and I intend," he adds, coolly, "to win."

" Not this time, not this," grinned Cresswell, showing his white ivories.

"Ay, this time !" observes his friend, coolly, with the air of a man accustomed to success. " Else Lucifer is not my guardian angel."

Well, it so turned out that Lucifer was not my lord's guardian angel this time, but another person was. For sure enough whilst they had been playing cards I had an opportunity of watching Calvert Cresswell's face, and, at the end of the examination, was more than ever convinced that it wasn't one a man would pin his trust to. Thou knowest what a fellow I am to believe in first impressions ? Well, when he made the bet with my lord, I swore to myself he meant mischief, and thou wilt learn anon, Harry, how right I was. Calvert Cresswell excused himself for a moment, and left the room, but it was not long ere he returned, bearing a tray with two glasses filled with spirits.

" The d——d servants are a-bed," he said,

setting one down before my lord, and taking one himself. "So I brought the drink in myself. Here's to success!"

Raising his glass to his lips, he motioned my lord to follow his example, but ere that gentleman could act in concert with his companion, I fell stumbling, as though by accident, against my lord's arm. The trick had the desired effect; the glass fell to the ground in fragments, and the liquor spilled.

"The devil take you for a d——d awkward rascal," yelled Cresswell, mad with rage.

"Take care," I returned, quietly and significantly, "only a glass is broken now; I may be tempted to break a head."

"Faith!" laughed my lord, "why, Cresswell, you're as mad as though the lad had spilled a poison instead of mere brandy!"

Cresswell paled, and forcing a laugh, murmured out an apology to me, and proffered his hand; I contented myself with bowing, and shortly afterwards withdrew.

Now, my first act, after I had left my lord and his quondam friend alone, was to seek out mine host, whom I found in the kitchen taking his ease, with a huge tankard of ale on a stool close by where he sat.

"Good evening, master!" said he, as I entered. "Can I do aught for ye?"

"Well, no—not precisely, that is, I want to have a gossip with you; but first, let's have a bottle of good wine."

"For yourself?"

"For both."

"But wine and beer is a bad mixture."

"Nonsense," I remarked, cajolingly:

> "Beer after wine, that drink is not mine,
> But wine after beer, is very good cheer!"

"Ah! larning is a prodigious fine thing," observed mine host, quite reconciled to the mixture I proposed. "I see you are a scholard, you are."

He was not slow in bringing the desired bottle, and, sitting down together, I made a very fine show of being vastly interested in every function, —social, and otherwise—of the village surrounding mine host's roof. The matter of our conversation was by no means thrilling, the fact will be well understood, when I tell you that pigs, cows, and the prospect of the wheat crop, were the principal topics.

"By the way!" says I, presently, very coolly, "where am I to sleep to-night?"

"Next to his lordship. It's a prodigiously fine room, clean as a whistle, and as comfortable as a forty-year-old widow with a jointure," returned mine host, smoking away, placidly.

"Couldn't you manage to change it, and give me another," I asked, feeling my way, very gently.

"Faith, master, with pleasure, I would," responded the plump owner of the inn, heartily. "But we haven't another bed in the house."

"H'm! I'm not sleepy," I observed, "and its just possible I wont lay down, to-night."

"By 'r lady!" ejaculated my companion, drinking a long draught of wine.

"You see, my friend," here I became deeply sympathetic and confidential, "I have a trust imposed upon me. You remember the gentleman who came in late?"

"Him with the black eyes, and domineering ways?"

"The very one."

"Ay."

"Well, I require you to put me up in a room next to his. Now, don't tell me," I added, as he appeared about to expostulate, "that you can't; but do as I tell you. It's for your own good."

"How's that?" demanded my fat interlocutor, crossing himself, and opening his eyes very wide.

"Well," I answered, carelessly, "altho' he's a particular friend of mine, he hath contracted a very pernicious habit."

"What's that?"

"He walks in his sleep!"

"Ah! that's nought," says the proprietor of the Wheatsheaf, as though relieved.

"So! you think nothing of a man, who, not only endangers his own life, with wandering about in his sleep, but, also, that of others?"

"By the mass, 'tis terrible! But, how so?" and again Monsieur le Proprietaire crosses himself repeatedly.

"My friend has a bad habit," I continued, off-handedly, "of walking in his sleep with a big knife, which he conceals about his person, with that cunning, for which somnambulists and madmen are notorious. He searches," I added, sinking my voice into a sepulchral whisper, "for the fattest man in the house, to kill him, under the impression that he is slaying a wild boar."

"Mother of God, save us!" cried the Papist (for mine host was a Papist, judging by his ejaculations) beads of perspiration dropping from his brow. "What is to be done? I am inclined to—to fattishness, myself."

"You are just the sort of man my friend would——" I began.

"What is to be done?" interrupted the other, groaning.

"Give me a room—a cell—a garret—anything next to him, so I may watch his movements, and prevent his committing——" once more I dropped my voice, and whispered in mine host's ear, "the crime of—Murder!"

"Oh!" cries he, "dear, kind gentleman, I will do anything. Your kindness deserves all praise, for 'tis a great sin, is murder. Certainly, I shall have the room next the sleep-walking gentleman's ready. I meant it as his dressing room; but it shall be yours," and, in great haste, muttering a variety of blessings on my head, he sped from the kitchen, leaving it entirely for me to enjoy a quiet laugh in.

After about a quarter of an hour's absence mine host returned, and asking me to follow him, showed me the way up two flights of steep stairs, through a narrow passage, and into the little room meant for my apartment. Mine host was considerably breathed, but whether for fear of having his throat cut by the somnambulist of my fancy, or the exertion of helping to hurriedly prepare the chamber for me, I cannot say. Be this how it may, it certainly was a fact that the space was a diminutive one; but I inwardly rejoiced at being next door to Mr. Calvert Cresswell.

"By the way," I said, just when the proprietor of the Wheatsheaf was leaving me, "what is the meaning of those holes up there?" For I noticed that about three or four feet above my head on the wall where I was standing, were about five or six round holes.

"Well, sir," answered the corpulent innkeeper, "we had some gay sparks here one night. One of 'em slept in this here room and two in the other. They got pranking or something; for in the night the gentlemen asleeping in this room ses as he had a pain in his inside, which no one believed, and wanted to wake the other two. So he said he couldn't get up, and so he jest took his pistol, and sent some bullets thro' the wall, instead of knocking at it to get help. But I'm sure there worn't naught the matter with him, and he did it only for devilry."

"Ah!" I observed, as though depreciative of the holes, although I thanked Providence for providing me with them, "some people might object to them. I should certainly have them covered up."

"I'll have it done to-morrow, sir," says my host, going. "Good night; and may the saints keep you, sleeping and waking."

"Good night!"

No sooner was the door closed than I took the only chair my room boasted, and stood upon it, and put my eye to the biggest of the holes. I could not repress an exclamation of joy. Fortune favoured me, I could plainly see into my neighbour's room, where a candle was burning. After this discovery I lost no time in finding my lord again, and bidding him and Mr. Calvert Cresswell "Good-night," went up to my little den and waited. One hour passed on, and I had almost worked myself into a perfect fever of impatience, when suddenly the door opened, and in strode my lord's quondam friend. Through the little loophole—which had been made by a reckless fellow in a reckless minute, and yet which afforded help to one of a more thoughtful class, which shows that good can and does often spring from evil—I espied all that he did.

I must confess to feeling some pangs of conscience for playing spy; but when I reflected that this man was capable of doing anything ill, and having the welfare of my patron at heart, I allowed no squeamishness to prevent me from finding out what Mr. Calvert Cresswell intended doing. That it was mischief on which he was bent I had no doubt. My unfailing instinct told me that.

When he entered his room he went straight to a mirror, and spent a little time in admiring himself; and I must do him the justice to say he was handsome enough to be vain. But he had no coxcomb's or fop's vanity. He was proud, but proud, like Lucifer, of his attainments, possessions, and looks.

"It's no use," he said at last, "playing against a man who has his master the Devil's luck like Hertford. I believe it is his very confidence that he is certain to win that makes others lose. He thinks he'll win the bet I made to-morrow. I'll take good care he doesn't this time, though. Fancy him finding out that Nellie Flouncewell was a spy. Ah! But it was not he that found her out; it was Ganymede, his student cupbearer, Jove's cupbearer. A meddling puppy," this was your humble servant, and I was scarcely flattered at the description of myself, "whom I'll run through the body one of these days. Ay, I will as soon as look at him. It is evident that the Devil sent one of his imps in the shape of this secretary of his, or something or other, to look after his beloved. Ha! but the imp isn't in the way now," he continued, going to one of a number of valises in a corner of the room. "To-morrow at White's the fellows will be saying 'My Lord of Hertford has lost a bet at last.' It will knock some of his infernal nonchalance out of him. I would give a couple of thousand guineas for that alone. Some fools say there is nothing so sweet as love. I say there is nothing so sweet as revenge. The qualities of revenge are more satisfying than those of love. Yes, my lord," he went on with a short, brutal laugh, unlocking one of his valises and taking thence a medium sized wooden box, "as sure as there is something to poison a horse so that when you have driven him for half a mile he will drop dead, so surely as my mother taught me to mix some poisons as subtle as those used by Catherine of Medicis, so surely shall you lose your bet, my Lord of Hertford."

So saying he opened the box, which held four or five bottles, and, selecting one, held it to the light. "There's enough here to do the thing," he went on, "and now for the stables to give my precious lord's horses their dose. Ha! ha! Bellamy," he laughed sneeringly, "who's the cleverest, the sleeping Solomon or the waking fool, I wonder?"

I waited not to hear or see more, but stepped from the chair, and with my shoes in my hand, glided noiselessly out of the room and down the stairs, nor rested till I had gained the outside of the stables where my lord's horses were; and here I put on my shoes. It was a glorious night, balmy and mild, with the stars shining in the deep sapphire sky, a night that would draw sweet songs from the soul of the poet, and from the hearts of young love. Being neither a poet or a lover just then, I took up a contemplative position, with my arms crossed, waiting with an expression of dreaminess, but with a wildly beating heart for the approach of the enemy. I turned the key—which I found sticking—of the stable door, after the fashion of a good old time-honoured proverb, and dropped it in my pocket, and presently when I heard footsteps I was aware that in less than two minutes I would be face to face with that false gentleman and friend, Calvert Cresswell.

He came along, whilst all but he and I seemed sleeping, as though in thought, with his eyes bent to the ground, so that not until he was quite close to me did he perceive that anyone stood there. He did not recognise me at first.

"Halloa!" says he, roughly, evidently taking me for a groom or stableman, "time you were in bed, my man."

"I beg your pardon, Mr. Cresswell," answers I, courteously.

"Who the devil are you?" he asks, angrily.

"My lord's secretary, at your service, sir."

"What are you doing here?"

"Like yourself, I humbly aspire to be an admirer of Nature as she sleeps. That is why I am here."

His black brazen eyes, with a flicker of hell's fire in them, look suspiciously at me. But my face is calm and placid I know. Besides, have I not the stable key in my pocket? Nothing tends to make one so virtuously calm as a feeling of security.

"You must be tired," says he, presently, a little more pleasantly. "Why are you not in bed?"

"If I felt disposed to be impertinent, sir," I answered, not stirring from the door. "I could ask the same question of you."

"Oh! I—I—am here," he returned, laughing uneasily. "To study nature—sleeping nature!"

"Oh, sir," I said with such a fine affectation of enthusiasm, that I astonished myself. "If I might be so bold, pray allow me to commune with you as to a kindred spirit, altho' mine be but a humble one!"

For this speech I fancy he immediately put me down as a species of poetical apprentice, which was just what I wanted.

"Let me tell you something," he said, with a sudden display of interest. "If you go to my room, on the left hand side of my bed, there is a bag with some wonderful books on Nature in it; if you like, go and fetch one, and I'll stay here and wait for you."

"Believe me, Mr. Cresswell," I observed, "I would rather hear knowledge from the lips of a man of sense and experience, than read it in the pages of the greatest writer who ever wrote." And I moved not from the stable door, and I saw him turn his hand in his pocket, as though the bottle were there.

"Aha!" thought I, "my fine gentleman, you'll not catch me tripping a measure to the time you play, I warrant!"

He did not appear quite at his ease after my answer, and looked at me rather suspiciously, but I maintained my assumed poetical demeanour, and was to all appearances star gazing

"It's a fine night!" he said at last, courteously. "I propose that we walk a little."

"With all the pleasure in life," I answered, with alacrity.

I moved from the stable door, and a shade of disappointment passed over his face. He saw that the key was gone. I could not forbear a smile, and we caught each other's eyes, and gazed into each other's faces.

"An odd idea struck me," he cried. "Do you know above all things I would like to see Lord Bellamy's horses. The notion is an excusable one you see," he added, with a charming attempt at frankness which would quite have deceived me had I not heard him give utterance to some very bad opinions in the room upstairs. "Because I am an owner of very good and successful horses, although perhaps not so fine as those his Lordship possesses."

"See! the door is locked," says I, turning the handle of the aforesaid, and indeed it was fast.

"No!" exclaims he, seizing hold of the handle in his turn, and trying to force the door open with all the strength of his iron wrist.

"Hold!" cries I. "Is it fair, Mr. Cresswell, that you should break the door which keeps another's cattle safe?"

"What do you mean?"

"Why, nothing, but that which I have said."

Calvert Cresswell remained thoughtful for a minute, and then shrugged his shoulders.

"Come, let us walk," said he.

And we did walk. I knew his tactics. He intended to tire me out, but not one Calvert Cresswell nor fifty such could have done so on that night. We walked and talked. He was bright, animated, and interesting for the first hour, and I tried to keep up with him in quoting from various standard authors, for I had no particular experience as he had to back myself up with. An hour flew by, and still we walked. He told me of his duelling adventures and his successes with the fair sex, which amazed and disgusted me not a little. "Surely," methought, "they must be foolish, indeed, to break their hearts over such splendidly empty, recklessly selfish, brute-hearted gentlemen as C. Cresswell." In after years I learned that women often mistake selfishness for resolution, hard-heartedness and brutality for "character." Ah well! it is "character" after all, but a very bad one.

We walked and I talked. A mist had risen,

through which the trees appeared like gigantic misshapen, shadowy spectres, and the nightingale was carolling forth the last notes of her night song. But I was not tired. Ever and anon my ccmpanion, with impatient looks he no longer took the trouble to disguise, asked me if I was not fatigued. I assured him solemnly that I was not; and, if I mistake not, he heard my statement with a curse under his breath against my holding out. I heeded not his fretting or his fuming; but, laughing in my sleeve, I played my rôle of the poetical apprentice to the life. We walked. A hundred times our footsteps turned up and down in the grounds around the stables. The twinkling stars grew tired before we did, and closed their bright eyes and faded away into sleep. We walked from night into that which is not day or night, and then the moon paled and sickened, and Aurora, rising from the sleep, opened her azure eyes, and smiled. Then lark and linnet began their song of praise, and all the Eastern skies were tinged with lovely blushes. Like the magnificent child of some glorious Titan, a new day burst upon us, with all the promise of a splend career. The flowers that had drooped at night lifted their heads, and whispered to eachother in breath so sweet that it perfumed the earth, that another day had come to them. It was well worth while to have stayed up all night to see the sweet and majestic beauties of nature unfold themselves. We walked, and my heart revelled in fresh breezes and the songs of the birds, and I felt as though I had rested the night through. Calvert Cresswell, however, looked wearied and worn. I called his attention to the lark's song.

"Oh! d——n the lark's song," cries he, thoroughly out of humour.

"The breezes, the flowers," I could not help saying, laughingly.

"To the devil with both!" growled my companion, who was really at heart no admirer of nature at all.

"You are tired," says I, hypocritically sympathetic, feeling, oh! so joyous; for the morning air was more inspiring than the finest wine. "Why not have a rest?"

"Have a rest, yourself, curse you," growls my companion again.

"Nay," cries I, "not on such a beautiful day. I thank you."

Seeing there was not the remotest chance of my turning in, Calvert Cresswell gave one last look at the stable door—which, curiously enough, I eyed too, and very sharply—and, with a peevish laugh, which was short, and half-a-dozen rattling oaths, he left me, to go back to his sleeping apartment.

No sooner had he taken his departure, than I burst out a-laughing, with such violence and enjoyment, that I startled the lark and the linnet soaring in the air above me. I never remember having laughed so much before. I would not have cared if Calvert Cresswell had heard me. I felt so strong, I could have felled an ox. Yes, triumph makes us all strong, and I was triumphant. I know I could have knocked Cresswell over, for all his boasted muscles and sinews, and his art and his science in that brutal art, called boxing.

Beneath the hypocrite's mask I had worn in his presence, there was a firm heart underneath ready to defend to the death my sleeping friend and patron. Cavalier blood, an old Puritan uncle of mine used to say of me.

In the midst of my merriment, a casement of the "Wheatsheaf" opened, and a head and shoulders came out. What a handsome, dissipated face it was that the fresh morning sun shone upon! What a mass of black hair fell on his shoulders; blacker still, in contrast to his white night dress, for he was only dressed in his night-gear, and, what is more, seemed to care no jot, who saw him so lightly clad. In his dark eyes, there shone the light of intellectuality, that no dissipation could quench. His forehead was lofty, white, and noble, showing, what the man really was, despite the surface of heedlessness.

"What the d——l art thou laughing at, Bellamy? Are these infernal roars thy early matins?"

"Just fancy, my Lord Hertford," I cried, "I have this morning caught a hunter in his own snare."

That same evening, at six o'clock, we arrived safely at the Castle; and two hours after, this Calvert Cresswell made his appearance in his coach. My lord waited for him on the steps to the entrance of the Castle, and gracefully extended his hand, in a sort of mock welcome.

"I told thee thou wouldst lose thy bet," he said.

The wager was paid, and then I told my lord what I had heard in the little room adjoining Calvert Cresswell's; now I am richer for five thousand pounds, and White's has expelled a member in the person of Calvert Cresswell.

This, my dear Harry, is the incident of which it pleases the fashionable world to talk so hugely about. After all, when matters of moment are sifted, they do not amount to much, do they?

From thine own, affectionate, and familiar friend,

Tom Bellamy.

THE WHITE PRIEST.

Millions of spiritual creatures walk the earth unseen, both when we wake and when we sleep.
Milton.

A healthy body is good; but a soul in right health,—it is the thing beyond all others to be prayed for.
Carlyle.

THE WHITE PRIEST.

PART I.

When Lady Fotheringay invited me to spend a few weeks at Fotheringay Castle in the autumn of 18— I accepted with pleasure, being overworked and brain weary, and lost no time in packing a few traps, and was soon on my way to the hospitable roof of my hostess, who was also, by-the-bye, a distant relative of mine. I arrived a good hour before dinner-time, and was shown to my room—there was always one kept in readiness for me—by an old butler, who had known me as a boy. This servitor was quite a character in his way, and was accepted by the servants as a sort of superior being. He was a cold, severe-looking man, with a clean-shaven face and hair austerely brushed; but he had a soft spot in his heart for one I knew—not for me particularly, but another. Whilst he unpacked my clothes I leisurely began the operation of shaving by the waning light.

"Is my lady well?" asked I, stropping my razor well, with my face covered with soapsuds.

"M'lady is well, Mr. Harwood," briefly responded Crisp, for such was his name.

"Is the house full?" I enquired again, in that peculiar tone which a man who is shaving can't help.

"Pretty full!" He began brushing a coat. Then he added, with sudden interest: "Miss Angela is well, and, oh! Mr. James, the most beautiful lady in the world."

Miss Angela Fotheringay was the only being in the world the surly old servitor loved. She was his idol and—mine. And although I was in holy orders my heart belonged to Angela, my hostess' daughter, and this Mr. Crisp knew very well. He liked to tease me.

"There isn't a gentleman who isn't in love with her," he said, and then left me to my own meditations.

When the first dinner-bell rang I descended to the drawing-room, and found Lady Fotheringay and some ladies and gentlemen whiling away the time before dinner in different ways. She received me, as her wont, with the utmost cordiality, and bade me sit beside her. The company did not impress me particularly. There were the usual languid, pale-faced, listless young men, and the same amount of whalebone-waisted, artificial young ladies to keep them in countenance. In one corner, under a huge palm, stood a bald-headed scientist expounding his doctrines to a tall and handsome man, who every now and again said "Ya-as, ya-as," as though he understood it all. One of the palm leaves tickled the scientist's bald pate, and every now and again the scientist's fingers would scratch at his bald pate until it was quite red.

The hum of conversation was at its loudest, when the door opened, and Angela, clad in white, entered. Never had I seen anyone half so beautiful, and so the rest thought, too, for first there came a hush, followed by a murmur of admiration. For beauty appeals to the dullest, where intellect and genius can appeal in vain. Lady Fotheringay looked with pride on her blooming young daughter, and who knows what schemes for her after-life flitted through her ladyship's ambitious brains. Angela laughed merrily as she greeted me.

"How very solemn you look," said she, as she pointed to my black frock coat and clerical-looking collar.

"Not so solemn," I returned, "but that your presence and laughter melts my heart into love and joy." Needless to say, this was said in a whisper.

Angela's beautiful cheek blushed a deeper hue, and I dared to think she thought kindly of me.

"By-the-bye, James," said her ladyship afterwards, "when you want to do any writing the library is always free. You will scarcely find anyone here now who will trouble the bookcase much." This she added with what may be called "society" sarcasm. Lady Fotheringay was a good-humoured, good-looking, and well-read woman of fifty or thereabouts, and a widow.

The dinner passed off as most dinners usually do, and the conversation was neither so brilliant nor animated that I need record it. Afterwards the ladies gave us a little music in the drawing-room, and even that little seemed too much.

Stay! maybe, the natural beauty of Angela Fotheringay made me draw invidious comparisons. Her very speaking voice was music methought. Why did those women sing, and so hush her? But the story of my love is not that which I have sat myself down to write. It is of something stranger—something sadder.

The day following my arrival at Fotheringay Castle, I had the happiness of walking in the grounds alone with Angela, and in her hesitation, her blushes and smiles, read, that her fresh young heart would be mine, if I proved myself worthy of her love.

The day passed like a glorious dream, so did a week after that, and then————and then Angela caught a feverish cold, and I was in despair, for they would not allow her to leave her room. Crisp (the surly old butler) informed me in so many words, that I had no business to take Miss Angela out in the grounds at such a season, and that it was my fault. I listened to him in gloomy self-reproach, and resolved to absent myself as long as compatible with the common laws of politeness, from the rest of the guests, until Angela recovered sufficiently to take her place amidst them. It was at this time that I bethought myself of Lady Fotheringay's invitation to go in the library when I wished to write. It was always free, she said, and the Castle was so full of people, it was really difficult to find a room, where one could have peace. The old library, I recollected, was pleasantly situated, overlooking the finest portion of the grounds, where the ancient trees grew thickest, and where the light laughter of the guests could not penetrate. I felt too nervous and wretched to read and write inmy own room; the library was just the place. Here, perhaps, Angela would come to see me, when they allowed her to leave her room; and, here I would tell her, perhaps, how sad and lonely I felt, during the time of her illness.

It was a dull afternoon, late in October, when I betook myself to the library, for the first time since many a long day. The surly Crisp, taking compassion on me, brought me the news that Angela was better, and might be allowed to come down afterwards, for a little while. I slipped a guinea into his hand, but, to my amazement, he put it back on the table, saying, quite deferentially for him:

"For anything else, Mr. James," he called me Mr. James when he was good-humoured, and Mr. Harwood when he was vexed, "but not for telling you Miss Angy (Angela) is better. You see, that news to me, was worth twenty pounds," and making a momentary feint of arranging the folds of a curtain, he left me to my own meditations, which were now joyful enough.

I sat near a table, on which several books lay, and I reached out my hand for one of them, thinking, by reading a little, I would become more composed; for the anticipation of beholding Angela once more, strangely unnerved me. In a haphazard way I opened the book, not caring whether it was fiction, travel, or science. It proved to be neither. It was the Holy Scriptures. In a dreamy way—yet knowing precisely what I read—my eyes rested on one of the Psalms of David, "I heard a voice from Heaven, saying unto me, Blessed are the dead——" I read no more, for suddenly I felt my limbs tremble violently, as if stricken with ague, and it was with quite an effort that I pulled myself together. "Surely," I thought, "I am not going to be ill." No; my pulse throbbed regularly and the beating of my heart was normal as its wont. The trembling passed over. I looked out on the dreary landscape; the leaves were falling thick and fast, and already the trees began to look bare and black in the cold twilight. I wondered what time it was, and went to the mantel-piece to consult the ancient clock there. But I fell back a step in surprise, for standing near the fire-place with his head resting on his left hand and his elbow leaning on the black marble, stood a handsome young man! I did not hear him enter the room, and I concluded that my mind was too preoccupied to have heard his footsteps. I noticed with no little surprise that his tall, elegant figure was clad in a cassock of dazzling whiteness, and that in his right hand he held a missal richly jewelled. His face was not only handsome in a pre-eminent degree, but possessed of a fascination and strength which even I was not proof against. His bright hair waved round his head almost like a golden cloud, and in his deep sapphire eyes beamed a steady light of nobility, ay, and suffering too, that made me think of the martyrs of old, nor can I tell why I thought so. His mouth was sweet and gentle, yet firm withal, and a peculiar smile hovered round the corners. It seemed to me that he repressed an inward agony; and yet I cannot assign any reason for thinking this. I wondered silently who he was, and then it struck me that he was a new arrival and his extraordinary dress a fancy one. I forgot to mention that Lady Fotheringay resembled Madame le Brun in her liking for theatricals, masquerades, etc. Charades were going on nearly every night, and it was by no means an uncommon thing to find a zealous "charader" promenading the Castle in his or her "get up" in the afternoon.

Attracted and fascinated, I bade the new-comer "Good evening," and reseated myself, hoping to have a conversation with him. He gently inclined his head, and seemed to wait for me to address him first.

"You are a new arrival," I observed, hesitatingly. "I have not hitherto had the pleasure of seeing you here."

"The Castle is not new to me," he answered,

gently, and I never recollect to have heard any voice like his before.

"Are you staying long?" I asked, almost timidly; nor can I account for this either, as I am neither of a timid nor nervous disposition.

"It depends."

"Have you been long acquainted with Lady Fotheringay?"

"Yes."

Although he answered briefly in words, his manner interested me more and more.

"You doubtless know Angela—Angela Fotheringay," I said, "and admire her?"

And I looked at him and thought with a pang of sadness at my heart how Angela must be interested in this handsome and fascinating stranger. How could I have a chance now. She would fall in love with him. I could bear comparison with most young fellows, but not with this extraordinary being. She would not be able to help herself.

The stranger seemed to read my thoughts, and a strange, sad, smile hovered round his lips, which touched me in an unaccountable way.

"I have seen Angela Fotheringay," he answered.

"But she has not seen me; and," he added firmly, "she must not. You must prevent her."

I marvelled more and more.

"You are vain of your appearance, and, unfortunately for me, with reason," I said, bitterly.

"Vanity has no part of me," he returned, looking at me with his penetrating and suffering eyes, which seemed to read my inmost soul.

"You are more than mortal, then?" I asked with something of scorn.

"I am the White Priest," answered the young man, gently.

"That may be," I observed, coldly, "and to-night if I were asked to take part in a masque, I should probably be 'King Richard, Cœur de Lion,' or, 'Rameses of Egypt.'"

"Come," said my companion, in a frank manner, "you look too kindly natured to be bad at heart, I wish to be on good terms with you."

"I have to ask your pardon," I rejoined, all my ill-humour evaporating under the magic of my companion's gentle and charming address. "I am—or was—jealous, and with good reason. But one thing strikes me as strange. How is it you are staying here, and yet do not wish Angela Fotheringay to see you? And yet again I beg your pardon. I really have no right to pry into your secrets."

He had not moved from the position by the mantelpiece, his beautiful head leaning on his hand; and I sat looking at him earnestly. I could not take my eyes off him.

"You are intended for the Church," he asked, presently. And when he spoke it was not as if my ears were addressed, but as though he spoke straight to my heart, and that my heart listened.

I nodded affirmatively.

"And you will be able to act deeds of charity, love, and patience, and then preach it to mankind; oh, fortunate man!" he exclaimed, in tones whose earnestness it would be impossible to describe.

"You are a born actor" I murmured.

"In life we all are," he said. "It is only after death that our spirits, freed from the masque of clay, become real."

At this conjuncture the dinner bell rang, and remembering that I had not changed my dress I apologised hurriedly and left the room, intending to resume the conversation afterwards, with my handsome companion. At the threshold stood a slight, beautiful figure, which I joyfully recognised as Angela's.

Seizing her delicate hand, I kissed it warmly, assuring her how more than happy I felt to see her downstairs again.

"Tell me, tell me," she cried, in a strangely excited tone, and not noticing my delight at seeing her. "Who is that young man dressed as a Priest, to whom you were speaking?"

In her agitation she laid one hand on my breast, and looked into my face with kindling eyes.

My heart sank, and groaned within me. "I knew how it would be." That accursed stranger had won her heart, by his extraordinary beauty, but seeing that excitement would only harm her, I smothered my own resentment as best I could, and soothed her, and told her he was a new-comer.

"Probably," I added, with pardonable sarcasm, "a wolf in sheep's clothing."

There were to be some tableaux vivants that night, and many guests had been invited besides those staying under the roof. I sat next to Angela amongst the audience, and never had I seen her look so animated and beautiful. Her cold had left her countenance a trifle thinner, giving it a more spirituelle expression. The curtains that screened the performers from view were drawn aside to some sweet music, and disclosed to the admiration of all beholders, a handsome young man dressed in white, holding in his left hand a jewelled missal, and with his head gently leaning on his right hand, in the same fashion as I had seen him do in the library. The limelight—for there was a raised platform, and everything arranged perfectly—shone full upon his fair, young face—showing it to the best advantage. The pose was excellent, and the figure almost matchless in its grace. Then applause burst forth, and I looked intently at the young man, and then at Angela, for the colour had fled from her cheeks, and she appeared sad and downcast. The clapping of hands, and the murmurs of approbation were at their height when I turned to the fair girl at my side, and said :

"What ails you, dear one ; tell me?"

"I do not know myself" she answered, sadly.

"But that man, that young man, is not the same one whom I saw speaking to you in the library." Then she added, shivering convulsively, and a hectic flush spreading over her face. "Promise me, promise me, James, that I shall see him again."

She had fainted, and I bore her from the place in my arms, and carried her to her mother's room, and gently placed her upon a couch. I did not leave till she had regained consciousness, nor was I asked to do so; and when at last she dropped into a gentle sleep, I whispered, "Lady Fotheringay, what was that tableau supposed to represent, that disturbed Angela so?"

"A foolish legend of Fotheringay Castle. A certain Priest is supposed to have committed some offence, and is doomed to wander through ages."

This is what Lady Fotheringay told me, and of one thing I am convinced and positive and that was *that the young man I had met in the library and the young man I had seen in the tableau vivant were not one and the same person!*

* * * * * * *

When I entered my bedroom that night, full of anxious and distracting thoughts, Crisp, the old butler, brushed past me. He threw open the door for me to enter (a most uncommon act of civility on his part) and assisted me to undress, with a sort of gruff sympathy in his manner.

"Good night, Mr. James," he said, at last, tucking me in, as he had done when I was a boy from college, and had come to the castle to spend my holidays.

"Good night, and God bless you, my friend,' I answered, sadly.

"God bless you, and have mercy on this unfortunate house!" he ejaculated. "And have mercy and pity on her so young—so young—so young;" and, with tears streaming from his old eyes, he left me to myself, and my night thoughts.

PART II.

During the next three days, I shunned the library, and wandered about the Castle like a restless spirit, in search of I knew not what.

Angela was once more confined to her room; not seriously ill, but suffering from nervous prostration. Her medical attendant said she had been allowed to leave her room too soon after her severe cold; and, that excitement had done her more harm than good. Crisp was my Mercury, and gave me news of my darling, almost every half-hour. I wrote her a little note, which my Lady Fotheringay took herself. When I met her at lunch time, my hostess gave me another, saying, with a smile:

"Angela is better. She has written you a few words, in answer to your note; and the naughty child would not let me see what it was. Here it is!"

She handed me a paper, folded in that intricate way, that only young girls are masters of, and turned to another of her guests, perfectly satisfied that her child was making satisfactory progress towards recovery. I opened the note with a misgiving at my heart, and read:

"Thanks, dear James, for your many kind inquiries. I am better. I shall come down this afternoon. I pray you to find out who that was you spoke to, the night I came downstairs. Believe me, it is not idle curiosity, that prompts me to ask this of you, but some feeling which I cannot account for. I pray you most sincerely and sadly, not to think me heartless, or cruel, or flippant. My whole heart is full of sorrow for you, and the injury I have done you, yet unwittingly.

ANGELA."

Crushing the paper in my hands, the room and its occupants swam round me, and I had to catch hold of the table, to save myself from falling. Now Autumn had indeed crept over the Summer sunshine in my heart, and I knew that Angela's love was no longer mine. Had she been other than she was, I could have met her rejection with scorn; for I am not one who can humbly love, without being loved in return. But she was so diffcrent to others! And did she not write: "I pray you most sincerely and sadly, not to think me heartless, cruel, and flippant?" Some terrible fascination held her soul enthralled; which, even I, man as I was, could not shake off. I allude, of course, to the young man I met in the library, whose name I did not know. I am happy in thinking now, that I nursed no bitterness against Angela, whose nature was so like her name; and whose flesh seemed more of air and Heaven, than earthly clay. One thing I was determined to do, and that was: to try and seek out the young man. Composing my feelings as best I could, I even managed to indulge in light conversation at table, wondering, in my heart of hearts, how I could do it.

At about three o'clock that afternoon, Angela, in a long white gown, trimmed with some airy lace, made her appearance in the morning-room, where her mother, and a few of the guests were sitting. She entered, leaning on the arm of Crisp, and followed by the maid, bearing a heap of white shawls. When she sat, or rather, sank into a large arm-chair, she was surrounded by a bevy of admiring sympathisers. She smiled, but, ah me, I noticed, not in her old, glad way; and although appearing to listen with interest, her large eyes continually turned towards me in a mournful way, quite unlike her former self. How bright and dilated her eyes seemed, and I remarked, with pain, that they were surrounded with black circles.

"Come here and join us, James," she cried at last. "Why are you sitting so far away? Have I a fever that you are afraid of catching it?" she added this with childish petulance, which would have sounded harsh in another but was charming in her.

I did not answer, but drew my chair nearer.

"Mother," she said to Lady Fotheringay, when the conversation had become pretty general, "I am going to claim that privilege always accorded to invalids, and ask one of you to read to me, and the rest to leave me. I am not amusing when I'm ill."

"But, darling!——" interposed her fond mother.

"Don't please think me disagreeable; but I want James to read to me," said Angela, "and, mother dear, look after our friends. Besides, I want to talk secrets," she added, laughingly.

She was a spoiled child, but as innocent and pure-minded as one of her namesakes. Alas! how soon the purest-minded are affected with deceit. Her light laugh deceived her mother, but not me; and, followed by the rest of the company, the good-natured mother withdrew, exacting a promise from me that I would not allow Angela to excite herself.

"You had my note?" she asked, timidly, when we were alone.

I answered "Yes," quietly; and she did not know how pained I was at the recollection of it.

"Have you nothing to say to me further?" she continued, hesitatingly.

"Nothing, Angela, nothing," I returned, with a little bitterness. "You have chosen an entire stranger to one who has known and loved you as a boy. So what should remain for me to say. All the words in the world will not alter it. All the love I offer will not make you return me any, since you love another."

"Oh! why do you not reproach me?" she

cried. "I led you to believe that I loved you, and—and—I did—until that evening. Heaven alone knows what has come over me. Before I saw—him—I felt so young, and now I feel so old," she added, half to herself, with a shudder. "James," she went on, earnestly, "listen to me. I feel I have not long to live; but before I die let me see him again."

She rose from her seat, and came towards me, with clasped hands, and a face whose expression I never can forget. It was illuminated in ecstatic recollection, and from her dilated eyes tears fell.

"Child! child! child!" I cried, sorrowfully. "You know not whom you love. He may be one utterly unworthy."

"It is not necessary to know those we love," she replied, hastily, through her tears. "For if he be unworthy, then my love shall raise him; and if he be more than worthy, why then—then he will raise me!"

How could I argue with this sweet unreason, even though every word she spoke stabbed me to the heart? I reminded her, noticing her increasing agitation, that I had promised Lady Fotheringay not to allow her to excite herself. Leading her back to her armchair, I assured her that if she left it again I would not stay longer. I eventually succeeded in soothing her, and promised that she should see the stranger again if I could arrange it. Half an hour passed away, and then Crisp re-appeared with an attendant sprite in the shape of Angela's young maid, with "strict orders" that Miss Angela must return to her room, as the doctor's instructions were that she must not remain up long. Of course, such infallible authority was not to be disputed; so, consigning her to the old servant's hands, we parted—she to bed and I to the library.

It was even a duller afternoon than the one when I had last paid a visit there. The old trees outside looked more like skeletons than ever, and the earth was melancholy and dark with the numbers of dead leaves which had fallen from them. "So fall all my hopes," I thought; "and the leaden sky is like my heart; and the only change it presages is winter and deeper sorrow yet."

I sat down, and took up the old Bible—this

time knowing full well what I did — and sought comfort and solace in King David's Psalms. : "Then thou shalt light my light. The Lord my God shall make my darkness to the light."

I had scarcely perused this beautiful verse, when a strange inner feeling told me of a presence in front of, and gazing at me. I became conscious of this even before I looked up. I knew the figure was near the mantel-piece facing me. I instinctively saw it was he, standing with his beautiful head inclining on his left hand, his elbow resting on the black marble, and holding a jewelled missal in his right hand. I felt that his eyes, with their steady light of nobility and suffering, that reminded me of the martyrs of old, were upon me. A smile hovered round his sweet and gentle mouth, which, yet withal, seemed to express an inward agony. I knew all this long ere I raised my eyes and met his look with mine. Then it was I noticed how different the other White Priest was in comparison to the one who stood before me. I allude to the tableau vivant of the White Priest, impersonated by Lord Walbrook.

No salutation passed; we dumbly recognised each other—at least, I did him. For there was something in his presence that drove all thoughts of jealousy away. There was an immeasurable distance between us, and I recognised and felt my inferiority.

I was the first to break silence. I did so brutally, humanly, and to the point.

"Angela has seen you, and she loves you," I said.

"Alas!" he returned in that voice I can never describe, and though the smile remained on his lips the expression of agony was more pronounced than ever.

"Something told me that I should meet you here again," I went on, doggedly. "And I came, without any intention of asking you who you are, to beg you to see Angela. If her love is fruitless, tell her so. She is young and beautiful, and could charm an anchorite from his cell."

"I may not see her; and I warned you to prevent her," the young man said, sadly.

"I am not God," I returned, sternly and abruptly. "She saw you without my help, and ere I could prevent her from doing so."

"Alas! unfortunate child," he exclaimed again, in a tone of anguish that saddened me, and made me in some strange manner pity him, as much as I did my lost love.

A pause ensued during which I felt myself attracted and fascinated towards this stranger in a way impossible to account for.

"I do not ask you who you are, nor from what place you come?" I observed at last, and instinctively I placed my hand on the Bible, with a prayer in my heart. "But tell me, can I help you in any way, that you seek me out, and not the others?"

"I was once a man of God, even as you are now," he answered me. "But youth and folly made me break a sacred vow I had sworn never to violate. My punishment," he added, "has even been greater than my crime."

There was something so awe-inspiring in his words and the manner of delivering them, that I dared not ask the nature of his sin. But of one thing I felt certain. He had expiated his crime, whatever it was. His face was not that of a damned, but of a blessed soul.

"Many years ago," he went on, and again I felt

as though my heart and not my ears were listening to him, "as I was going out one morning, a messenger came to me and told me a young, beautiful woman was on her deathbed, and wished to confess a great sin to me, and receive absolution and comfort. I had promised to make one of a pleasure party; yes, and I, a Priest, refused to attend the last dying moments of a woman, and perform the rite of anointing her in her last moments! I told the messenger I would attend her, when I returned. When I did return the woman was dead; but previous to her death she had written her confession, and sent it to me by the same messenger, who advised me of her departing soul. I looked for the manuscript written by the woman's trembling hands, but in vain. I searched everywhere, and enquired of the messenger where he had placed the confession. He told me that he had put it into this jewelled missal, which was laid in this room. I looked into the missal, but it was not there. Some invisible agency had taken it away, and since then I am doomed to search for it, but still I have not found it. Now you know my offence, and my punishment."

"I shall find it for you," I said, at last, in a

voice so hollow that I could not recognise it as my own.

"I thank you, my friend," said my companion gently, and looking at me with his mild eyes beaming with almost a divine love. I do not know how it came to pass, but I rose and went to the door, for I did not wish to see in what manner he left the apartment, and lo, and behold, a light figure came to me with a cry of "I have seen him again, and oh, how fairer than a king's son is my love."

It was Angela!

She laughed a light rippling laugh, but it was terrible. Her eyes shone with a sort of fever, and her cheeks burned as though a fire consumed them. She followed me back into the library. The White Priest was gone.

"Why did you leave your room," I asked, almost sternly ; "and how comes it that you in your ill health should be permitted to do so?"

"I sent Janette away," she made answer wearily, disappointed to find the stranger gone—"I sent Janette on an errand."

"A pretended one," I interposed, ruthlessly.

"So be it then!" she continued, sadly. "I do

not know why I love this man, but I love him; and loving him, I cannot exist without seeing him. God nor Heaven can be angry at the pretext love makes to see those we love."

Then I recollected one of Rochefoucauld's maxims, as I watched the poor child in her love delirium. "In their first passion, women love their lovers; in all others they love love."

I saw that her affection for me had been but a girlish fancy.

If Angela thought her absence would be unnoticed for any length of time, she was mistaken. She was presently fetched away by Janette and Crisp, who assured me, they had been searching half the Castle for her. She retired with them, reluctantly enough.

I was no sooner left to myself, than I began a search for the lost confession, that my strange visitor had told me about. Filled with a vague belief, that it was my lot and destiny to find the lost document, I began to look about me, with unabated zeal. But, cupboard, bookcase, shelves, and desks were ransacked in vain; there was no sign, even, of anything approaching a confession. After another hunt, equally unsuccessful, I began to give it up almost in despair, but for an unforeseen incident. In violently opening the drawer of a little desk, near the oak wainscoting, my elbow came sharply in contact with what seemed to be the head of a nail. Stopping in my efforts, to rub the injured arm, what was my surprise and amazement to behold, that the head of the nail was really a spring, and a part—about a foot—of the wainscoting had flown open, disclosing to view, a very dusty interior, like a small cupboard. The Castle was an old one, and at the time when it was built—centuries ago—secret doors, traps, etc., had been the fashion; these, in later years, had been fastened down, and, I suppose this little one had been overlooked. With a presentiment that I had gained the object of my search, I thrust my hand into the darkness, and, thence, drew forth, amidst some ashes and rubbish, a roll of parchment. Regaining my composure, after some moments (for the find made me giddy and trembling) I unrolled the top of the scroll. It was headed thus, word for word:

"Ye Dyeing Confessiones of Mary, Ladye Hudspethe, inne ye yeare of oure Lorde, A.D. 1053."

I dared to read no more. Curiosity, before this

terrible mystery, retreated abashed. I know not, what inexplicable and inevitable power brought me to find this manuscript. I accepted it without desiring to dive deeper into that, which was beyond human power to understand. I have merely undertaken to state facts. I do not pretend to solve the occult.

Crisp reminded me, when I retired to my room to dress, that there were to be another series of tableaux vivants that night. I had forgotten the fact. It seemed as though I were walking about in a dream. Indeed, I would have thought so, since the occurrence in the library; but the parchment with the confession was real enough. I folded it and put it in my breast pocket. When I joined the company in the drawing-room, my hostess anxiously inquired about my health. She remarked:

"How pale and worn you look, James."

I assured her my health was never better, to which she added:

"Ah! you mustn't worry about Angela. The doctor says she has only a protracted cold, and will soon be well again."

* * * * * *

There was a larger audience than ever to witness the night's tableaux. The fame of the last had spread, and all who were honoured with invitations, came with alacrity. The principal feature was Lord Walbrook's impersonation of the "White Priest." Everyone was talking about it, and now everyone of distinction (and some without any) came to witness it. Distinction came (for a wonder) early, so as not to miss this particular tableau. Distinction rustled to their places amid a cascade of laces, perfume, and the glitter of jewels. Distinction came with a pleasurable flutter of excitement, dying—it murmured—to see the dear, the charming man, "Lord Walbrook." Distinction was not disappointed. It rarely ever is. Ruined hopes, and the like, are the portion more or less of the commoner herd. Distinction lifts up her dainty dress, and trips lightly o'er those snares and pitfalls, which her humbler brothers and sisters fall headlong into. But I digress. I am not writing a dissertation; therefore let me finish the episode, which is the saddest in my life.

The room in which the tableaux were given was, as I said before, crowded to excess. It was a particularly large chamber, with a gallery and a stage, and formerly kings had been entertained there. It was, in fact, the finest apartment in the Castle, and held upwards of eight hundred people. Soft music played a prelude to the tableaux, and on the tiptoe of expectation, amidst a universal hush and darkness, the curtains were drawn aside, and disclosed to view the figure of the "White Priest." There he stood, in his usual pose, holding the jewelled missal, and his head gently inclined in a thoughtful attitude on his hand. Yet there was something in his face that held my heart and soul spellbound. I gave a hurried glance at the audience. Those nearest me had paled, and the laughing, glittering mass of humanity might have been dead people for the movement and sound that they emitted. It was the silence, not of a listening public, but like death. The suffering on the priest's young face was strongly marked, and it seemed to me that he repressed an inward agony, even as when I had first seen him in the library. The same steady light beamed from his deep sapphire eyes, that same light of nobility and suffering, which made me think of the martyrs of old. Something,

I know not what to this day, seized me. Like one who walks in a dream, I found myself near the platform, and, drawing forth the confession from my breast pocket, held it to the White Priest. It was taken—how I know not—and my lips murmured:

"Thou art not the false priest. Take this, and may the Lord remember no more the sins and offences of thy youth."

And lo! a look of loving kindness swept over the stranger's face. The smile of agony was cleared away, and supplanted by one such as I think the happy immortals wear, and the anguish passed away from his eyes, as he answered and said:

"We shall meet again!"

"We shall meet again in Eternity," my heart responded.

Just then I heard the light step of a woman and the rustle of silk and lace. I looked, now bereft of the power to move or to cry out. The rustling garments and light step were—Angela's. How had she come there? Who allowed her to come on the platform? I know not to this day—save that she was magnetised there as I.

She moved like a beautiful somnambulist towards the figure of the young White Priest. An indescribable beatitude beamed from her face, and her eyes were wide open, intense and heavenly. She appeared to be almost transparent in her etherealism. When she stood within a yard of the stranger she stretched forth her arms, as though to clasp him. Then, with a sigh like that of a grieved child, she exclaimed, still as if she were asleep: "I come! Yes, I come, oh, my beloved!" and fell forward to the ground with scarce a sound, so light had she become.

* * * * * *

A noise awoke me from my stupor. I heard a voice saying:

"Who has been taking my part? I've just come, and find someone else has been filling it."

It was Lord Walbrook, who had arrived late, dressed for the tableau vivant as the "White Priest."

* * * * * *

There is a grave, over which stands a broken marble column, indicative of one cut off in youth and loveliness. At the base of the column is chiselled the single name of **Angela**. If tears and deepest sorrow could have called her back she had been here on earth again, as fair, as sweet as ever.

She sleeps undisturbed by sorrow and unavailing love—not in the dark mausoleum of the Fotheringays, where even death assumes a chillier aspect, but in the softer bosom of Mother Earth. Ay, softer than many hearts beating with life above it. Winter and summer, fresh flowers are placed there by loving hands, and I visit the spot even as pilgrims visit the shrines of their saints. When oppressed by the world, its vanities, and vain glories, I come hither, and, over the tomb of this once lovely child, learn the mutability of all things, and my heart is softened by thoughts of the past. Fortune otherwise has favoured me, because, merely to forget, I worked with patience and perseverance, which led to success, as it always must. I am a bishop now, and shall go to my grave with no other recollection of a woman's love but that of Angela's. Far away I may meet her and— him, as he promised me.

But one word more and I am done. One warm evening in June, as I went to her grave with a bunch of white lilies, I was surprised to see an old man asleep on the ground, near the base of the broken column. His face was hidden by his arm, and his hair was quite white. I knelt down by his side, intending to minister such consolation as his condition demanded and my calling and humanity gave. I could get no answer to my questions, so I gently moved his arm. It was Crisp, the old butler, and he was dead. In life divided from his fair child-mistress, he thought in death to be united.

Farewell!

WHOSE WAS THE GUILT?

A SKETCH FROM REAL LIFE.

Robes and furr'd gowns hide all. Plate Sin with gold,
And the strong lance of Justice hurtless breaks.
"King Lear."

Few . . have virtue to withstand the highest bidder.
George Washington.

The progress of rivers to the ocean is not so rapid as that of a man to sin.
Voltaire.

WHOSE WAS THE GUILT ?
A SKETCH FROM REAL LIFE.

Mrs. Farquahar sat in a reverie, awaiting the arrival of her lord and dinner. Judging by the contraction of her brows, she was troubled, and judging again by the pursing up of her small red mouth, she was angry, aye, contemptuously so. But, troubled or angry, there could be no doubt in the mind of even a casual observer, that she was a very handsome young woman. Handsome, with that peculiar beauty belonging to Cleopatra, when she was called "The Serpent of Old Nile." In form, she was long, lithe, and fairly well-covered and her hair was of a peculiar shade of russet brown, with more than a dash of red in it. Good natured people said that it was dyed: but those same sweet-natured people could not detract from the beauty of her face; every feature of which seemed chiselled. Like many other handsome people, her profile was infinitely better than her full face, and the former she always preferred to show; knowing—like a clever woman—her "good points."

"He's always late!" she said, presently, apostrophising her absent spouse. "I am getting, oh, so tired of him! Oh! that I were not tied to the fool! He'll never make his way, like other men. If I were free, I believe Lord Fetherhed would marry——"

Her soliloquy was at an end; for her husband entered, and soon after, dinner was served.

Farquahar seemed a good sort of fellow in his way, and handsome too, but he was a man's man, and his wife looked down upon him with scorn. She was a woman whose nature demanded worship, and he was a man whose caresses, two years after marriage, filled her thirsty soul with loathing. He kissed her as a child does a pretty toy, and her whole heart rebelled against it. She had wished to be all, and found herself but a quarter. She wished to be treated like an idol, or an Empress, and she found herself treated only like a superior sort of animal.

They had now been married eight years, and

each day they drifted farther and farther apart. When they met, they sparred at each other like cat and dog. They had neither, any sympathy for the other. They stayed together, because the law ordained that they must. Oh! wise law, that makes two people, united but in hate, to live together. Oh! noble law of an enlightened country, that forces two hearts to beat together the tune of agony and discord, until either death or dishonour part them.

It is said that people should not marry, unless they love each other. But, granted they do love each other when they wed, neither knows how the other will turn out after the ceremony. The gentle girl is often a Xantippe in disguise; the kind, good-humoured man is often nothing but a libertine and brute. And finding each other out too late, those two unhappy beings must eke out their miserable existence together; knowing no hope of freedom exists for them, but crime or death! It is horrible, and it is narrow, to know that there is no way out of a luckless marriage but disgrace, or the tomb. Oh! sage Law-givers, when ye deal with Mankind and Morals, know, that half the cause of vice and crime is naught but your own doing. Repeal the Laws, and cleaner and happier cities will be yours, to rule.

But to return.

"By the way, Jenny!" observed her husband as he put on his Inverness cape, preparatory to starting for his club. "You might put the brake on, regarding young Fetherhed. The fellows at the club are beginning to talk about it. It looks so d—— bad for——"

"You, eh?" sneered his wife.

"No, both of us," he answered, good humouredly.

"Well!" she responded, "do I tell you what the women tell me, about you and Dolly Varcoe, the music hall girl?"

The man coloured ever so slightly, and answered, hotly:

"She's honest as the day, would you were half as pure!"

"You idiot!" cried Mrs. Farquahar, bursting into a strident laugh. "Don't I know you men? Why, you are all ready to swear to any woman, no matter how bad, as long as she has conferred her favours on you."

He left the house with a curse, his wife's shrill

laughter echoing in his ears, as he banged the street door.

Mrs. Farquahar returned to her little boudoir, and, changing her attire to one of spotless white, (emblematic of her own lost innocence) stood in front of her glass, arranging her hair, so that it should look negligent, without appearing unkempt. She took an imitation diamond coronet from her wardrobe, and put it on her head; for, although tolerably well off, and possessed of some diamonds, she had neither riviére nor tiara.

If she had looked handsome before, certainly, she looked doubly so now, with the shimmering glass in her wealth of lovely hair. She looked in dreamy admiration at her own image, and then the imitation coronet of diamonds melted away, and in its stead, she saw a real tiara, and her little boudoir was exalted into one of purple, gold, and fine linen, instead of the pretty tapestry.

"Lord Fetherhed!" a discreet voice spake at the door, and, as the owner of the title entered, Mrs. Farquahar seized the imitation diamond coronet from her hair, and threw it to the corner of the apartment. Her maid ushered the visitor into the room, and closed the door quietly upon the two.

"What have you done?" cries the new comer with more warmth than one could have imagined from so exquisite a looking personage. For his figure and face were as expressive as a tailor's dummy. And this young lord loved this woman of many ways and means.

"What have I done?" she repeated, taking the two hands held out to her. "Why, I have thrown aside my false diamond coronet as an unworthy thing to see you in!"

It was a Machiavellian stroke, and quite worthy of the ambitious and unprincipled woman.

"You shall have a real one!" lisped the young man, who had never known what it was to have his own wishes thwarted. "By Jove! what a shame that you should not have everything you want."

He was quite moved to pity about it. She followed up her attack.

"What does it matter—a paltry diamond coronet?" she asked, in deep and earnest tones, with her fine eyes upraised to her companion's face. "I can never have what I really want."

"What is it?" he asks, magnetised.

"How can I tell you that it is your love, true and undying love that I want?" she returns, as though with an effort.

"You have it, darling."

"No, no, no!" she answers. "We must part. To live with you in the sight of God and the world as your mistress would but break my heart; for the thought would be always haunting me that you would leave me."

"If you were but free," groaned out the young dupe. "I would dispel your doubts."

"Would you marry me?" she asked suddenly.

"Heaven is my witness that I would!" he responded, with the ring of truth and love in his young voice.

"And you would allow neither your father or family to separate us," she cried, excitedly.

"No; nothing in the world, my love; as there is a God!" repeated the young man solemnly; for he had not learned blasphemy, and the name of the Creator still remained for him the holy word before which he had knelt so many times in the chapel at Eton—not so very long ago after all, poor lad!

* * * * * *

Miss Dolly Varcoe, of the Frivolity Theatre, London, was seated at her breakfast at two o'clock in the afternoon, at her house in St. Paul's Glade, when her maid announced that a lady wished to see her.

"Tell her I'm in bed—asleep—dead—anything," says Miss Dolly, with her mouth full of ham and eggs. "I'm not going to see any ladies, you bet."

"I would, miss, if I were you!" her Phyllis remarks, with that familiarity for which theatrical ladiesmaids are remarkable. "It might be for your good."

"Show her up," is all Miss Dolly deigns to say. For she does not pay her maid : although perhaps her visitors do.

Miss Varcoe hears a light step, and she sees before her a well-dressed woman, with a bright, smiling face. Dolly is good humour personified, and catches the infection, and smiles back.

"Miss Varcoe?" says her visitor, interrogatively.

"The same!" returns Dolly, bowing in a burlesque fashion ; for she sees her visitor is accustomed to the usages of polite society.

"I am Jenny Farquahar—Ned Farquahar's wife," Mrs. Farquahar continues, for it is she.

"Now for a scene!" thinks Doll to herself, falling into a chair, preparing to hear vituperations and hysterics.

But nothing of the sort. Little by little she is won over by the wonderful influence this woman wields, and is prepared to do anything for her. By degrees the hours steal on, and still they chat, but it is in a whisper; possibly they fear the walls will hear them.

"He does not allow you much," remarked Mrs. Farquahar, as though pityingly.

"No," answered her companion, frankly. "I am head over heels in debt."

"Would fifteen thousand pounds be any good to you?" demands the visitor in a lower voice.

"Would they?" almost laughs the other. "Try me and see."

"By the way, does Ned still take chloral?" queried Mrs. Farquahar.

"Yes; when he can't sleep," replies the other, starting.

"Sometimes more than other times?" Jenny Farquahar persists.

"I don't understand."

"Does he vary his doses?"

"Yes."

"Do you wish to earn fifteen thousand pounds?" asks Mrs. Farquahar, with a parched throat.

"I do."

"Then," says Mrs. Farquahar, sinking her voice into a still lower whisper, "the next time Ned takes a dose and does—not—wake—fifteen thousand pounds are—yours!"

The two women stare into each other's eyes. At last Dolly says, with a bitter laugh:

"I'm only a man's plaything. Why shouldn't I be the death of one? For one it was who killed all that is good in me. And one may as well be dead—as bad. It shall be done. Now go."

* * * * * *

A week later the following paragraph appeared in the papers:

"The body of a well-known member of society was found in the house of Miss Dolly Varcoe, the burlesque artiste. The deceased was in the habit of taking chloral, an overdose of which killed him."

* * * * * *

Twelve months after Ned Farquahar's death another paragraph appears in the papers, under the heading of fashionable marriages, setting forth how Lord Fetherhed led to the altar Mrs. Jenny Farquahar, widow of Edward Farquahar, Esq.

Does crime always get punished? On the stage, yes; but in real life—well, not so often. For Lady Fetherhed is a respected and admired member of the fashionable world, with a blazing tiara of real diamonds in lieu of the paste ones; and Dolly Varcoe? Dolly is simply the head of her profession.

Now that I have recorded these vulgar facts of three vulgar people, there remains one problem I would like to have solved myself. To you, oh! grave and reverend seigniors, seated on earth's judgment seats, I apply for justice. I would ask you which of the three sin-workers was the most guilty? The first sinner is the husband, who, by his reckless conduct and indifference of the sensitive organisation of his wife, killed her heart. The second is the wife, who, driven into the arms of another, instils a crime into another woman's ears; and the third is the young woman, whose soul at an early age was trampled into dust by man, and who, to avenge and enrich herself at one time, slew cne of her destroyers. Who was the guiltiest? Rulers and magistrates, ye can determine causes and administer justice on actions; but the inward workings are lost on you. These are things beyond your power—beyond that of earth's wisest men. But there is One who judges, not the evil act alone, but that which caused its existence; who judges not the surface of things, but that which is hidden from man. That judge is God!

THE DYING PROFESSOR.

A SKETCH.

"He shall not die, by God!" cried he. The Accusing Spirit which flew up to Heaven's chancery with the oath blushed as he gave it in: and the Recording Angel as he wrote it down dropped a tear upon the word and blotted it out for ever.
Sterne—"TRISTRAM SHANDY."

The world's a bubble, and the life a man
Less than a span.
Bacon

L

THE DYING PROFESSOR.

A SKETCH.

When Dr. Claudius Frühling, the most eminent professor in the whole City of Berlin, entered the great hall to deliver his lecture, the vast concourse which thronged the building, rose as one man, and greeted him with enthusiasm. He was young indeed to be so learned and popular a man; barely thirty years of age, and possessed of a weird intellectual handsomeness, far more striking than mere physical beauty. His black hair was brushed away from his lofty forehead, and contrasted strangely with the extreme pallor of his face. His steely blue eyes seemed to emit sparks, or, as one of the students said, had a touch of "hell's fire" in their abnormal brightness. Even the long lashes that surmounted them, cast no shadows over their brilliancy. When he stood on the platform, and they had shouted themselves hoarse, they noticed that he was paler and thinner than usual.

"He is overworking himself," they said, carelessly among themselves, then, in breathless silence, waited for the young master to begin.

Dr. Claudius Frühling, standing on the platform, looked hurriedly about him. Ere he commenced, a young giant, over six feet in height, with the golden, curly head of an Apollo, and the swelling neck of an ox, approached him.

"Are you suffering?" he asked imploringly, in a low voice, touching the Professor's wrist, blue-veined and delicate, with his mighty hand. The touch was as gentle as that of a child.

"I am well, Karl, I am well," responded Dr. Frühling, testily. "Sit down, cannot you see the people are waiting for me to begin?"

So the student returned to his seat, wondering much at the master's querulous tones. Karl was a wild admirer of the Professor's. Like him of old, his love for his friend surpassed that of women. It was the triumph of mind over matter: of mental power over physical. Had it been a question of strength he would have stolen fire from Heaven, like Prometheus, to lay at the shrine of his idol. That man in the glorious pride and intoxication of youth, whose muscles were powerful enough to have broken iron bars like daisy chains, had the mental capacity of a child. The Professor's learning completely quelled the power and desires in the body of the Herculean student. When the students assembled at their "Kneipe," drinking their "bocks," Karl, with his strident voice, would shout "Dr. Claudius Frühling" as a toast, and woe betide any student who left heel-taps, or was tardy in responding! The Professor had an affection for this student. He loved to walk into the forests with him, and watch him break huge boughs off the trees as though they were twigs. Sapient men shook their heads, and wondered why Dr. Claudius had not chosen one of them to be his friend. But the Professor loved Nature as well as Science, and admired the glow of health on Karl's handsome face, his well-knit form and sunny hair.

To-night the young man, quick to notice every change in Dr. Frühling, was seized with some vague alarm, which did not diminish even when the master began his lecture.

"My friends," said he, "I am here to-night to discourse to you on the Heavenly bodies. Now I am about to tell you of a wonderful one which I discovered last night."

How eagerly all ears strained to catch each sound so that not a word should be lost. Wonder upon wonder. Dr. Claudius Frühling had discovered a new world, perhaps!

"Last night," continued the learned Doctor, passing his delicate fingers across his brow, which was wet with an icy perspiration, "ere I went to my bed I gazed from my open window into the blue sky above me. How cloudless, clear, and serenely beautiful it was! It seemed as though the world were dead, and the Heavens were in mourning for it. Ay, and the many stars were the tears shed by Angels for this Universal Death. Oh, my friends! How many, and how strange were the thoughts that beset me! Then it was that my eyes rested on a planet that I had never seen before. So bright and beautiful it was that I could but stand in silent ecstacy over its brilliancy. Suddenly it grew larger and larger, it seemed to open, and I saw——"

Here the Professor paused, overcome with

emotion. His audience listened with admiration that was not unmixed with surprise; and the student Karl sat as though frozen to his seat.

"I saw," continued Dr. Claudius Frühling, in a low, earnest voice, "I saw a new world open before me. A new world, my friends, of wisdom and beauty, compared to which mundane arts and sciences are as nothing."

The audience looked more astonished than ever. Was the Doctor laughing at them, or was he really in earnest? But hush! he spoke again:

"My friends," and now his voice sounded faint and beautiful as melody borne upon the summer wind from distant hills, "in that star—exists—another world. I am convinced—that—the only perfect wisdom is there. Oh, my beloved! How dark and unfathomable all was to me before. How plain and clear—all is to me now. We are all children, and the only great teacher is—Death!"

He gasped—tottered—then fell into the student's outstretched arms, for Karl had leaped on to the platform to save him.

"I will hold thee to earth. Heaven shall not

steal thee from me," cried the student in a hoarse strong voice, as though he defied Heaven's might.

Then with a smile of deep content, the Professor's soul shook off its tenement of clay, and soared into the realms of eternal light.

Yes, Dr. Claudius Frühling, the most eminent master of Art and Knowledge in the whole City of Berlin, was dead. Dead, as any ordinary and unlearned person might be.

So it happened whilst the City throbbed with excitement at losing so great a personage at so brief a notice; the herculean student, Karl, wept his maiden tears for the loss of an adored friend.

Right in the heart of the town, Berlin has erected a cold marble monument to the memory of her learned doctor. By this, men will remember him, till the stone falls to pieces with rot and decay. But the student needs no monument to remind him of his lost master, for right in the centre of his warm young heart, love has erected a cenotaph that crumbles not with Time, nor fades with Death.

THE TWO BROTHERS.

Revenge, at first though sweet,
Bitter ere long back on itself recoils.
" Paradise Lost."

Forty thousand brothers
Could not, with all their quantity of love,
Make up my sum.
" Hamlet."

THE TWO BROTHERS.

A TRUE AND TRAGIC HISTORY WRITTEN BY ME, NOW FATHER BERTRAM, SOMETIME COUNT BASILIUS OF ALTENBOURG. IN THE YEAR OF OUR LORD, 1405. THE FAITHFULNESS OF WHOSE STATEMENT, WITNESSETH MY IMMORTAL SOUL.

Right willingly did I consecrate my life to devotion and prayer, yet, oh my soul! not ere I had found out how bitter life was beyond the cloister walls; how full of shattered hopes, and how poor and fruitless the highest ambitions were! I saw life once, and loved it as a child would worship the appearance of Dead Sea Fruit. Then, deluded by its false loveliness, I tasted of it (how I pity myself for it, now) and lo! naught but bitterness, even as of myrrh and aloes, remained in my heart. Once I was surrounded by gay companions, libertines, and courtesans, and they painted the Monastery as a place to be shunned. A living tomb of dust and ashes. Yet, I say now, better it is to live in dust and ashes, than die in brightness and beauty, that hath no depth, no truth, and no stability in it.

The outside world is like the Dead Sea Fruit; and the Cloisters are its ashes. There is fair falseness in one, and grey truth in the other. Yet hold! 'tis not of myself that I wish to write now. Sometimes in my meditations and fastings come the thoughts of past times so powerfully upon me, that I think it would ease my mind in no small measure to write down that thing which so sorely troubleth me. Yet again, 'tis not of myself that I wish to write. My former self is buried with my past; and so long hath it been dead that I could no more disturb it than the ashes of the dead.

It was in summer time some years ago that I first came to this cloister. The fame of its Superior had penetrated Altenbourg, the place from whence I came, and I, wearied of a life of so-called pleasure, shook off my courtiers and lemans, and freed myself—Ay! freed myself, as I had never been freed before, in this little narrow cell. No more would I hear their hated flattery. No more could they, Judas-like, betray me with their tainted kisses. In this narrow cell I sank on my knees—I, the once-powerful Count Bertram—and thanked Heaven for having given me strength to gain my freedom; for, indeed, rulers have none. The greater the despot the bigger the slave. For he who worketh most iniquity and injustice against people must necessarily be a servant to fear and mistrust, and also a prey to a tormenting conscience. He who is allowed to do what he lists must naturally do wrong sometimes. Without being wickedly inclined, I had sinned much, and right glad was I to be able to devote myself to something new—prayer and inability to do wrong. The Superior, Father Anselm, was a kind but stern man. He soon evinced a liking to me, and I became one of his favourites. After I had been there for six months he sent for me, and asked me how I should like to have a pupil. I told him I should like to teach a lad very much, particularly if he were to become the head of a people. "For," said I, "I would teach him to learn what I had learnt too tardily, to rule myself in all things first, and then to govern my people afterwards."

The Superior approved of my answer, but said, shaking his head,

"The stripling I would have thee teach, my son, is, indeed, destined to command, and yet, —and yet, I fear me, that he is a lad who will not so easily be led."

Two or three days after my conversation with the Superior, I was introduced to my pupil, whom I will now describe. In stature he was tall and lithe, yet well-knit withal, with a countenance at once striking and handsome. His black hair hung down each side of his cheeks, and fell in natural curls past his shoulders, affording a striking contrast with the pallor of his skin. His eyes were black and flashed already his passions forth like one twice his age. His eyebrows were long, and of a raven hue, and by a curious freak of nature, seemed to be as one black mark across his open and commanding brow. Yet this seemed rather to add than detract from a certain mysterious beauty. His nose was of the shape of an eagle's beak, and the nostrils dilated and distended like those of a high-spirited horse, when he became angry. This, as his preceptor, he never was with me. His name was Lord Achillas Vilmão Falcondale, the only child of noble parents, both living, at the time he came to me. He was haughty and cold at first, and treated me —although I was, or rather had been, of a finer family than he—as though I were his menial. As he grew to know me better and when I had explained the most difficult parts of Euclid to him, and initiated him into the mysteries of many dead languages, he respected and esteemed me for my knowledge, which was not mean, even amidst scholars. Ultimately he looked upon me in the light of a friend ; aye, and as a loved and only one to boot. With friendship came confidence, and he imparted to me many things concerning his parents.

"My sire is stern and warlike," he said, "but, my mother is a wondrously gentle lady."

More than once I saw the haughty Lord of Perilous Castle pass the cloister on his charger, followed by a train of goodly knights. He was a man of about forty years, and his son strongly resembled him ; but youth softened the lad's countenance, whereas, the other's prime had hardened it. More than once, too, in going to visit the sick of body and mind, I had met the litter of the fair Lady Falcondale. She had each time stopped to thank me for my instructing her son, and ordered her servants to give me money for my poor. Pale, and beautiful, and sad, she was ever. The gossips said she had married her lord to please her father, altho' she loved another at the time. Ah me! 'neath her sweet smiling lips and tender eyes, I knew a heart was breaking; I knew the son was rarely at his mother's side. "It fatigues me to sit amidst her ladies," he told me once, "they are wearisome with their eternal spinning and tapestry making, or they giggle and chatter like senseless magpies. When I sit alone with my mother, she weeps, and I pity her, but cannot understand her grief. Sometimes she looks at me with her blue eyes, oh! so pitiful, and then they fill with tears, and lo! she hastily leaves me. Women are strange creatures," added the boy, unconsciously repeating a truism. "I prefer to hunt with my hawk kestrels and herons. Would that I were old enough to go to the wars, and add lustre to our honoured name, as my father says I must."

Companionless, save for me, the dark young lord went his ways, and so wondrous were they that the foolish folk would say that he had learned to commune with the Evil One, and that I had taught him.

In truth he was a strange lad to those that knew him not. Sometimes, in my goings and comings from and to the cloister, and my vocation called me out in all sorts of weather, I would catch sight of a tall, lithe figure on the top of a huge boulder of rock, in the midst of a wild scenery, whilst the elements were at war with each other; and this figure I knew to be that of the young Achillas. He would watch the angry sea dash against the foot of the rugged mass of stone whereon he stood with his arms crossed, as though he were indeed some dark spirit defying the mighty powers.

The peasants coming from the market crossed themselves when they saw him, and fled precipitately.

"He holdeth communion with the Devil," they said amongst themselves, and allowed him a wide space accordingly. Once he moored a barge that let water, and when it was sinking, although the waves were running high, he threw himself amongst them, and only succeeded after great difficulty in reaching land. In vain I besought him to seek less dangerous pastimes, he listened to me gravely and respectfully, and asked:

"Was there not a time, oh my father, when thou wert even so wild a creature as I?"

"Aye," I made answer, "but in truth, my very dear son, experience hath taught me how foolish I have been."

"Then, my father," returned the young lord, laying his big, strong hand protectingly and lovingly on mine, "let experience teach me too, as it did thee. Alas! save of thy wisdom, I know my turbulent heart cannot learn aught else."

He learned much, and so well, that I could see the time not far distant when I should be able to impart no more book-lore to him. His favourite hero was Alexander the Great, and him, he said, he would emulate, although I told him his passions were too strong to be a disciple of that justly celebrated leader.

One day when he came as usual to take a lesson from me, and we both walked along in a grove after the manner of the Greek teachers, taking all species as subjects for discussion and dissection, I noticed my pupil, instead of being attentive as his wont, was distracted and gloomy. In vain I waited his erudite or enquiring remarks. They came not.

"What aileth my son to-day?" I asked with surprise.

"Nothing, my father, nothing," he replied. "Thou, with thy knowledge, wouldst laugh did I tell thee."

"Nay, neither as thy instructor or friend would I do so," I observed.

Seeing how earnestly I wished him to unburden himself to me, Achillas spake:

"This morning when I came down betimes, Althea, my mother's favourite lady, came to me with a smile on her saucy lips, telling me my mother would speak to me in her chamber. 'I will attend her this moment,' quoth I, nor could I restrain myself from adding disdainfully at her wanton manner, 'Would that my lady mother did not love such foolish creatures as thyself.' 'Ungallant!' replies the Lady Althea. 'Better 'tis to be foolish like I, than heartless and austere like thee,' and away she went, this time with no smile upon her lips. I was not slow in going to my mother, whom I found in her chamber on her prie-dieu alone. My spurs and sword clanked as I entered, and she turned, almost with a shudder, towards me. I kissed her hand and she saluted my brow, yet with something, methought, of fear in her manner. Presently she fell to weeping hysterically, and threw herself at my feet, bathing them with her tears. Alarmed and horror-stricken at seeing my mother thus, I raised her, and tenderly placing her on a couch, implored her on my knees to tell me the cause of her grief. 'Promise me,' she moaned, 'swear to me, my son, by the Blessed Virgin, not to kill that which is born to me.' These astounding words first made me doubt her reason, but, after awhile, when she became calmer, she told me that a saying ran through her family that—

'Vaska's last, a woman fair,
Will a Cain and Abel bear.'

My mother is an Italian, and of a noble family, called Vaska. She was taken to England when but six years old, and is the last of that line. I left her to come to you, father, quieting her by saying I should ever cherish either a brother or a sister if I had one. This is the cause of my uneasiness and distraction, for, as I left, labour pains were upon her."

"Poor lady!" I observed, when he had concluded, and he looked moodily before him. "But take heart of grace, women in her condition have always strange fancies. Thy gentle mother is no exception, so fret not thy soul, my son, without any cause."

"But tell me," I asked, as a sudden thought struck me. "Could'st thou love a brother or a sister?"

"Aye!" answered the young lord. "With all my soul. More than aught else."

Even as we spoke, we had wended our way towards the end of the grove which led to the Castle. It was a lovely spring day, and the flowers yet glistened with the morning dew. Every wind that fairy-like danced over the trees and grasses teemed with a fresher life, and breathed on the world like a new Creator warming all into life from the chaos of winter. Even as we wandered on, a messenger with a troupe of pretty damsels at his heels came towards us. He and they were breathless with running.

"Joy! joy!" he cried. "The lady Falcondale hath a son, my lord, and you a brother!"

"Joy!" repeated the young lord Achillas, taking his plumed hat from his head, and looking towards the heavens. "May God grant it so!"

They heeded not this strange answer, but with bows and curtsies passed on to bring the news elsewhere. The words of my pupil were echoed by me in my innermost heart, and I prayed long and deeply for the house of Falcondale that night.

Time passed on with swift wings, and some months passed ere I saw my pupil again; he was in deep mourning, but a light shone in his bright eagle eyes I had never seen there before. He told me in a low voice that the gentle lady of Falcondale had died two hours after the birth of her son, but that the child lived and throve, and that he had been christened Angelo, in memory of his mother, whose name was Angela. I asked my pupil if he loved the little one, not from curiosity, but because I yearned that he should do so. Strange to say the old doggerel of a couplet concerning the last of the Vaskas had haunted me. My doubts were speedily dispelled; now I knew what that new light meant in his eyes, it was love, for his voice was full of joy as he said :

"Ay, for once, forgive me, father, I am sincerely thankful to God for sending this angel to me. Now I have something I can and do truly love. My mother with her dying breath commended him to my care and affection, for my father is at the Holy Wars, and I promised her departing soul to protect and love him ever. Ah, my father, you must see him, for he shall be your pupil too when he is older. You must see his blue eyes, like those forget-me-nots that grow in the brooks, and his locks of hair as golden as the daffodillies in the woods. I know he will be sweet and obedient, and never, like I, cause you a sigh and a prayer. Already he knows me, and when I enter his room he holds out his little arms, and makes as though he would come to me."

I could scarcely believe my senses! Was this the stern, dark young lord who spoke? His whole countenance seemed changed, as he discoursed of his young kinsman. Time went on, months and years flew by, I saw my former pupil less and less frequently. His father, the old lord, had received his death wound in the Holy Wars, and sent a message to his son, as the eldest, that he should uphold the honour of his race, and war too against the infidel, who would desecrate all that which is most holy.

I heard strange tales of the Lord Achillas' doings. He was sterner than ever, and his dark doings filled all with awe. His retainers and people held him in terror, all but the young Angelo. For the lightest offence he would have them dreadfully punished; although on the other hand, he was insolently generous; and would scatter gold amongst them like chaff. His austerity was remarkable, and he was obeyed in fear and trembling.

Once he sentenced a poor vagrant to be scourged, and afterward to have his right hand cut off for stealing a measure of corn, because his sick wife was starving. Then, ere the sentence was carried out, a little lad, with blue eyes and golden locks, who had been listening, threw himself on his knees before his stern kinsman, and, with streaming tears, begged mercy for the unfortunate mortal. Like Saul of old, the evil spirit was charmed away at the sight of his beloved, and raising him in alarm that his beautiful eyes should be dimmed with tears, not only promised to revoke the sentence, but gave him money to give to the hapless man. He so loved this fair young brother, that at night, the lad's old nurse averred, that she saw the dark Lord of Falcondale lean over his bed—his black hair mingling with the other's golden curls—murmuring words of love, like a mother to her sleeping infant.

It was not long before Angelo became my pupil, and, as his brother had prophecied in the early days, he was docile, obedient, and lovable always. It is true he had not the abnormal gifts of Achillas, but he was a pleasant scholar, and I could find no fault in him. He excelled more in the lighter arts, and charmed all by his sweet singing, and playing on the lute; his brother disdained these accomplishments for himself, as effeminate, but in Angelo he thought them glorious and beautiful. Although the younger of the two brothers often stayed the elder's hand from wrong-doing, he was not always present to prevent the ills which accrued from Lord Achillas' austerity. The younger was as much loved as the elder was feared, and the invitations which the surrounding noble houses dared not extend towards the elder, were sent to the young Angelo. This made him absent sometimes, and when he returned he would invariably find someone suffering for incurring the wrath of his brother.

Still, the lord was magnificently generous, and his people and retainers were better housed and fed than any other lord's. Not one of the passions possessed by Achillas belonged to the blue-eyed Angelo. I heard that not one, but many hearths had been ruined by the Lord Falcondale. Neither the name of wife or maid bore any holiness for him. The one that for an instant his eye rested on was ruined. Some said it was the fascination of a dove for a serpent. The title of libertine was not his. His victims were more to blame than he, seeing how they sought him, and he not them. Some whispered he worked terrible spells, learned of the Devil to bewitch women. Be this how it may, nothing on earth was so prized and loved as Angelo by his brother. When Angelo was eighteen, the

Lord Achillas was about thirty-four or five, and acceding to his younger brother's earnest desires (who thought to calm the elder's roving and restless spirit), he wedded a lady of beauty, wealth, and title in London, then brought her to Castle Perilous.

I was present with many other ecclesiastics on the occasion of the arrival of the bride and bridegroom to their home. How well I remember that day! All was made as gay and beautiful as possible to greet them. For, on a feast day, what rigour will not be forgotten by the peasantry? Grievances were put aside, and men and women donned their best attire to welcome their lord's home-coming. Everything was propitious and smiling, save the weather, and that was dull, and moreover it drizzled a fine, disagreeable rain. The priests and Angelo waited on the covered terrace. The young man was greatly elated, and the excitement added a new lustre to his eyes, and new colour to his cheeks. We looked at him in amazement, for his beauty was God-like. Amidst acclamations and shouts the Lord Achillas Falcondale arrived, and helped his bride to alight from her litter, and led her to the terrace where Angelo stood. He embraced his brother with passionate eagerness, and I saw at a glance all the love and devotion of his wayward heart belonged only to the fair-haired stripling.

"And how doth my boy fare," asked the lord, fondly, stroking the shining locks of the younger, for he had doffed his hat, and awaited to greet his sister-in-law. "Ah! the air of Norfolk, and the hunt here hath given thee a rare colour, and thine eye is so bright that it will raise havoc in the heart of every dame."

Thus spoke the haughty heir of Falcondale, but only Angelo and I heard him; for by reason of my long acquaintance I was the only one who closely followed my younger pupil in greeting the elder. Then came the introduction. She was beautiful indeed, this new-made bride, with her black tresses and bright brown eyes that looked as though they could love and hate with equal intensity. Indeed, she was not unlike, as far as feminine softness would allow, her husband himself. When she gave her hand to Angelo he looked at her and started. The colour faded from his cheeks, and she—she paled too. The lord noticed this in his brother though not in his bride.

"Ho!" he cried in his deep sounding voice, "a flagon of wine here, my brother is faint. Lean on me, dear one," he added in a low voice, giving his arm to Angelo. "I see well that these accursed merry-makings have made thee ill. Thou hast worked too hard. That flush and now that pallor. I will have the leech for thee instantly."

"Nay, 'tis nothing, dearest, kindest brother," gently said Angelo. "Look to thy wife—the Lady Sabine."

But the wayward elder almost carried the other within, leaving his bride standing mortified with her attendants on the terrace. She was fain to accept my escort, and she and her ladies were shown to their new home by me.

"A strange home-coming, father," said Lord Falcondale's wife to me, sadly. "Rain on a bride denotes misfortune. Pray for me, my father." She knelt on the threshold, and I gave her my blessing. But there were presentiments in my heart that filled me with sorrow for the house of Falcondale.

Two or three months afterwards, during which I had heard or seen nothing of Lord Falcondale or Angelo, strange stories came to my ears concerning them. It was whispered that a day after the marriage, Angelo had begun to shun the society of his brother and his bride, and so marked was this that he rose before anyone else of the household and returned late when all were abed. They said, too, that the Lord Achillas Falcondale was sterner and gloomier than ever; for he grieved about his brother, and his young bride wandered neglected in the Castle and over its grounds.

One day, as I sat alone, someone entered in on my solitude, and I glanced up from the weighty tome I perused, to see---Angelo! His fair face was thinner than when I saw it last, and the colour had fled his cheeks. His eyes were strange and wild-looking. Altogether unlike my beloved pupil's mien was this.

"What is it with thee?" I asked, surprised and grieved at what I saw.

"Father," exclaimed the young man, clasping his hands and speaking as though he were choking, "listen to me, or I shall go mad, and advise me ere I lay rash hands on myself!"

I besought him to calm himself, nor would I listen until he sat down, and could tell me his sorrow more rationally. This I did for his good, seeing how enfevered his young blood was. Ah, me, as I saw him thus, my life's blood, too, leaped into something like action neath my solemn cassock. He told me the following in such a mournful voice that it seemed no longer that of the gay Angelo.

"You know, father, that ever since I first set mine eyes on my brother's bride, I have avoided her, ay, and him, too. For, according to thy teaching, beloved and honoured instructor, I would not cast mine eyes longingly on another's treasure, and that other's that of my noble brother. For this reason I have risen earlier than the lark every morning, and have gone away so I should not return till late at night, when all should be in bed. O! turn not your sainted eyes from me," (here the lad's voice faltered, and I quailed as the noble youth bent his knee to me, as though acknowledging my superiority, which, in truth, I was far from feeling), "for I love the Lady

Falcondale as my very soul! Yester-morn I rose to flee away so early from the Castle that the sun had scarce begun to rise when I trod down the stairs. Scarcely, however, had my hand touched the bolt of the gates when I felt my nervous fingers in the iron clasp of someone. Ay, it was my brother! He looked worn and grieved. 'Why dost thou fly me thus, my Angelo?' he said in gentle tones, which made me feel doubly how great a villain I was. 'If I have wedded, 'tis not because I love thee less, for my love for thee is above the love of woman. What more can I tell thee? What can I do to show thee that my wife hath not usurped thy place in my heart?' How, after these words could I tell him the truth? I had rather have killed myself than done so. And he said he had been watching my comings and goings, till he could bear no longer. How unworthy his noble love I felt when he grieved over my changed condition. He caught my hands in his, and, for the first time in his life I know, he wept. Yes, the dark, stern Lord of Falcondale wept silently over me, and said: 'My brother, oh, my brother!' Never was there a love like his! Never a devotion to compare to it so pure and selfless. He prevailed on me to return to the Castle. 'Thou shalt want for nought,' were his words. 'Sabine shall sing to thee in thy hours of weariness, and I will read to my boy.' Sabine, father, is his wife, and noted for her beautiful voice, as well as for her personal beauty. Release me, my father, from these fetters of roses that will lead me to crime, advise me how to act," concluded the young man, "or I must die."

I spoke to him for some time, and succeeded in cheering him, and he left me with a lighter step, promising to quell the passion. Alas! I had heard such vows before. Had they been kept? But few, I fear me.

A month after the foregoing, I was summoned to the castle by Lord Falcondale, who stated that he wished me to guard a treasure of his, whilst he went to the Holy War in pursuance of his dead father's wish.

I arrived at the Castle, and saw my lord on the terrace. He was sitting in a great chair, with his head leaning on his left hand, in a thoughtful attitude, and his right hand in his favourite position, on the hilt of his sword. By his side, on a lower chair sat Angelo with his lute. I greeted them both, and Lord Falcondale said:

"Father, in my absence, will you, in your unfailing watchfulness, guard my treasure well?"

"Where is the treasure, my son?" I asked.

"My golden one, here," answered the future Crusader, pointing to his brother. The latter started, and seized the elder's hand.

"Let me go with thee," he pleaded, earnestly. "I will do anything, and obey thee in all. Take me as thy foot-page. I will groom thy horse, and nurse thee if—but Heaven forbid it!—thou should'st be wounded."

The elder smiled.

"Think'st thou," he cried, "that thy white tapered hands were meant for aught but to touch the lute and write madrigals for women? Nay thou must stay at home and look after it, and take heed," this grimly, "that my wife goeth not a-gadding;" adding earnestly: "I would not have thee exposed to danger, for all the honours that are in this world."

I promised to do all I could for Angelo, and not many days after, the Lord of Falcondale took his departure with a goodly train of knights for Palestine.

* * * * *

Six years elapsed, and the fame of the Lord of Falcondale's valour in the war against the Infidels spread through many lands. In a certain triumphal entry into a besieged city, and whilst he rode at the head of a great army, with his countenance so severe and stern, even in its handsomeness, that the inhabitants all fell back awed and afraid to look upon it, a fair-haired lad chanced to stand in front of a crowd. The Crusader's eagle glance fell upon him, and in a strange voice he bade him stand forward. Blushing and confused the youth obeyed.

" Here is gold for thee, boy," said the Crusader, and turning in his saddle to his troops he spoke in a mighty voice, so sonorous that all did hear.

" Give ear unto me, gentlemen and hirelings, if either of ye despoil one person or one single dwelling in this city, that one man or band shall instantly suffer a terrible death."

Then a great shout of joy arose from the multitude, and they blessed their noble conqueror. " Noble chief," said the lad who had received the

Crusader's gold, and emboldened by the curiosity of youth, " would that I knew why you have so mercifully spared us and our city, when your hand is said to be so merciless and cruel ?"

" It was for one Angelo's sake, boy," the Lord of Falcondale made answer, a smile flitting across his proud countenance, and as quickly dying away. " For thou resemblest him much in person. May thou be pure and spotless like him in mind. Adieu."

This incident in a terrible and tumultuous career was told me by an eye witness.

Six years passed away, as I have written before, and still the Lord of Falcondale had not returned, but in truth I saw but less and less of Angelo, who appeared now as he would avoid me altogether. He spent much time away from the Castle, and I often marked the Lady Sabine alone on the terrace, surrounded by her ladies, they at work and she idle, but with a smile of contentment on her face. What had produced this strange happiness in her ? However, I neither heard or saw anything wrong going on between Angelo and the Lady Sabine, and I was lulled into the belief that all was as fair as it appeared. At last a day came, and oh! my soul is full of horror at the recollection of it! It was in this wise. At four o'clock in the morning as I was returning from sitting watch at the bedside of a poor dead woman, I saw a bronzed knight on a charger, unattended, walking his horse slowly along the road.

"God bless thee, my son!" I cried, as I noticed the red cross on his arm, and saw in whose loved cause he had fought.

"I thank thee, dear father Bertram, but tell me how fares my golden treasure," said the Crusader.

"Welcome!" I exclaimed, joyously, "I see now that thou art my pupil, the Lord of Falcondale. I knew ye not at first."

He was of a certainty, pleased to see me again, but a heavy cloud hung over his brow.

"I have disbanded my train, and am going home alone," he told me, " but thrice has my horse stumbled in coming, and my heart misgives me sorely. My steed hath never failed me before. All the time I have been away, my heart hath not fallen once, save when thinking of my forsaken Angelo. Tell me that he is well?" he asked eagerly.

I assured him he was so, and, pressing me sorely, I at length yielded in accompanying him to the Castle. If I had followed my inclinations, and some strange foreboding in my own heart, I would have said to him prophetically, "do not go."

The Castle looked as though it were wrapped, like the inmates, in slumber. He had a secret way in which to enter, without disturbing the servants, and together, we presently stood on the threshold of his noble halls; previously having taken his steed to the stables.

"Now, I pray you, let me return," I said, for some strange fear took possession of me, but he would not hear of it, and besought me to remain.

"Come," he whispered, "'tis to Angelo's room we will go. His lips shall be the first to press mine."

With hurried tread he led me on, through rooms and corridors, whose rich furniture reminded me of my Castle of Altenbourg. But I knew that happiness dwelt not there any more than it did here, and it was with an unmoved mind that I saw the greatest splendours that taste and wealth could purchase so lavishly distributed in every nook and corner. We passed silently through the picture gallery, where hung the portraits of the Falcondales. Here, on giving an involuntary glance at his mother's picture, Lord Falcondale paled and trembled violently.

"Look!" he cried. "Is it my fancy, or is it true? It seems as though she would weep!"

"Mine eyes see naught but a handsome picture," I returned. "Thou art weary, my dear son, and thy enfevered fancy gives life to that which in truth hath none."

"Come then!" he exclaimed, "it may be so!"

Leaving the gallery, we saw two cloaks, a man and a woman's, thrown together on an arm-chair. This time I shuddered. But he did not notice it, and hurried on in a feverish haste. At last, we gained Angelo's room. He entered on tiptoe, I following. He went to the bed, and turned to me, pallid to the lips.

"He is not here, father! Is he dead? Tell me the truth!" he exclaimed, hoarsely.

The bed was empty. Angelo was not there.

"Mayhap he hath gone to London, my son," I

observed, gently. "I have told thee he is not dead."

He breathed a sigh of relief, whilst my heart sank lower and lower.

We departed from his younger brother's chamber, and descended to the corridor where his wife's apartment was situated. I would have left him there, but he detained me with a strange force, which I had no power to resist. A greater force impelled me to stay, nor can I attribute this to anything earthly. As we advanced — he always as leader—he hesitated as he drew very gently aside a heavy curtain that served as a door to the room. We both stood frozen in our places, he with his eagle eyes flashing terrible wrath, and a sardonic smile on his lips, I half forgetting my priestly vocation and transfixed with horror and amaze. From the darkened room came a voice, voluptuous and soft, but distinct and clear.

"Oh, how I love thee, my beloved," said the voice, "thou art so constant in thy kindness, so changeless in thy love. How far above all other men thou art! How can my heart compare thee, my loved and loving soul, to that cold, hard tyrant now happily away from us? 'Tis false to say that women love those that are most harsh to them! It may be for the soulless. But I—I had a soul, my own, ere thou didst take it away from me. In thine eyes-light my heart expands, as the flowers do in the sun. I breathe, I live, I feel, yet all my senses are thine. I am not more myself, and thou, oh, thou hast a double being—mine and thine together!"

As in a dream, it appeared that the Lord of Falcondale's hand was on his sword's hilt, and I rushed forward and clasped his arm.

"Stay, stay," I cried, hoarsely, "not murder for that dear God's sake. It is—"

He shook me off ere I could utter the name, and rushed in the apartment with his sword drawn.

* * * * * *

Words are too feeble to describe that terrible moment. His unerring arm, accustomed to do deadly work, failed not this time.

When I followed him I entered into the apartment of the dead.

* * * * * *

Not I—not he, spoke a word. The silence must have lasted nearly a quarter of an hour.

He was the first to say, sternly and without emotion,

"Mine honour is avenged, for which not God, the King, nor England will blame me."

"But whom have you slain?"

"My wife!" he answered, "and her accursed paramour."

I drew aside one of the heavy curtains that shut out my God's light from that room of blood, with a dire presentiment in my heart.

A terrible cry burst from the dark Lord of Falcondale's lips, such a one as will make me shudder in my grave. For the sun shone in on the love of Achillas' life. A fair, young, upturned face met his gaze that would smile on him no more. The floor was stained with a crimson stream, one drop of which the Lord of Falcondale would not willingly have shed to save his own life.

The prophecy was fulfilled, the last of the Vaskas had borne a Cain! Angelo was dead! Slain by the hand of him who loved him dearer than life.

* * * * * *

Years after, a messenger brought me a letter from a foreign land. From this letter, I take but a few lines.

"I am dying, dying, ere I have thoroughly expiated my crime. My spirit, I know, cannot rest in peace. Commend my erring heart unto Heaven, oh, my father! this from
"Thy dying son,
ACHILLAS."

How long, how long, oh, my soul! will he wander restless o'er the earth? For, methought I saw him yesterday—not—not in the flesh. His eyes, were the eyes of one who hath solved the mystery of Life and Death, and drunk deeply of the cup of sorrow. I pray most fervently on earth, oh, my Lord God! for his salvation and peace. And, should I once go to Heaven, there will I intercede for my poor son, for evermore, until he shall come.

And the truth of what I have told, witnesseth my undying soul, and, if I have lied, perdition will seize me in eternity.

(Signed)   FATHER BERTRAM,
The Cloister of St. John, in the Year of Grace, 1405.

Some Press Opinions

ON THE FIRST EDITION OF

SEVEN STORIES,

By Helene E. A. Gingold

"Vanity Fair," 24th August, 1893.

Miss Gingold here faces the public in a new character, telling us seven delightful stories. The art of writing a good short story is given to few, but Miss Gingold has proved seven times that it is her's. We have noted her work in these columns before, and we have now to record fresh talent displayed in new fields. The author's apology for the short story, that it ministers to the needs of those busy people who have no time to read long books, is not altogether needed; for the general reader wants both short and long tales to charm his various moods, and the greatest abundance of the one ill supplies the absence of the other. Shortness is the lustre of story-telling, for in a short story the matter less obscures the manner, and art is the more obvious. We see this in these stories. Throughout the book the personality of the writer is never apparent. "The Rabbi of Moscow" is full of that poetic mysticism which belongs only to the Jews. To attempt to bring Father Abraham down a flight of shining steps in a vision is to run no mean risk. But the author succeeds, and produces a tale that is at once strong, simple, and beautiful in pathetic truth. "Veritas" is a metaphysical story, wherein the human mind and passions are exposed with originality and insight. Its end, where the man who has prayed that Virtue may be universal grows fearful and wants to undo his granted wish, is really clever. "The White Priest" is among the best ghost stories we have read. Then we have a sporting tale of the last century, the narrator of which, one Tom Bellamy, a man of sound old English character, tells his tale with the sturdy, honest ring of that stiff-necked, wholesome time. 'Tis an olden-time sporting story, and a good one.

In this tale, however, the reader is struck by two pieces of carelessness, which, no doubt, will be remedied in future editions. Calvert Cresswell, the villain of the story, is described as being "a pretty frequent visitor at my Lord's house"; while he has been expelled from White's for his endeavour to swindle "my Lord." And although Tom Bellamy is recounting an obviously recent event, he says that "in after years" he learned to alter an opinion formed during the happening of that event which is described as "now the talk of the town." These are but small faults—slips rather—yet can we find no greater errors in this volume; wherefore to point them out is, in itself, to highly commend Miss Gingold's newest book.

Besides a short but strong German character-sketch, we have also "Whose was the Guilt?" wherein is set forth one of the most serious questions of the day, that of the marriage-tie; which forms the basis of a tragic story. "The Two Brothers" concludes the book, and is a mediæval tale of much importance, both in character painting and in portrayal of powerful passions. Our author is a strong enough local colourist to be able to bring her scenes, with no discoverable effort, forcibly before the reader.

To conclude, we cannot help wishing that in the next book of stories that Miss Gingold writes we may find some that are told by female characters. Her avowed object is to amuse, and in this she has certainly succeeded. So far as we are aware, this author has done nothing better than these *Seven Stories*.

"MANCHESTER COURIER," 2nd September 1893.

This young authoress has already secured such warm admiration for her former works, consisting more especially of poems, that she scarcely needs the approbation of the critic But the "*Seven Stories*" are most powerful and original, artistic and charming. That the late Duke of Saxe-Coburg-Gotha expressed through his secretary the profound interest and appreciation with which H.H. read both the novel and the verses of this lady is not astonishing. For he was well able to enjoy the clever descriptions and highly realistic talent possessed by the writer of the "*Seven Stories*," each of which presents remarkable originality, each of which is so condensed and so striking in its manner of narration. I should single out the " White Priest " as the most dramatic and extraordinary of the series. But all are good, and Miss Gingold thoroughly understands the art of producing the now very popular " short story," which is either very bad and unsatisfactory, or, as in the present case, quite a work of art, full of interest and suggestion, and well furnished with "local colour," not long enough to weary, and not short enough to balk the appetite of the cultivated reader.

" THE JEWISH WORLD," 18th August, 1893.

Miss Hélène Gingold had no pretentious object in view in giving her latest work to the public; nevertheless, we are much mistaken, if its humility be not forgotten in the entertainment it provides. " I did my best," she says, " not to instruct and enlighten, but to amuse, and if I succeed in diverting the work-harassed brain, be it but for one short hour, I well know that these humble stories have not been written in vain.' We would not flatter ourselves so much as to claim a prominent place among the work-harassed brains, but certainly these stories have afforded us a certain amount of relief.

" *Seven Stories* " traverses considerable ground and treats of manners, whose existence were separated by centuries. " The Rabbi of Moscow " is a story of long ago; " Veritas " will suit all time; then we have a story of last century. Hurriedly, then, we are brought from the realms of gross vibrating humanity into the world of mysticism; and hardly less rapid is the transition from these regions to surroundings in which " The Dying Professor " once lived and breathed. Again we are taken on the wings of the wind and find ourselves partaking of the life of the Crusaders, silently philosophising on their acts and their temptations. Throughout all these tales, however, as we read we detected a pervading strain of sadness and there is betrayed on the part of the writer an inclination to dwell upon the wickedness of human kind, and its misery, especially that which comes of love betrayed. We speak not here of the love of man and woman only. For Miss Gingold speaks of the love of man for man, of Jonathan for David—love which passeth that of a woman.

Only one story, the first, is of special Jewish interest, and that deals with an episode all too common in our history—the Blood Accusation. Nevertheless, there is added to its recital the charm of the writer, and that alone would suffice to relieve it of its platitude and commonplace, The keynote is rung upon trust in the guardian power of Providence, for in this instance the fell machinations of the Czar's favourite Radamoff are defeated by the interposition of Father Abraham himself. Rabbi Solomon is a loveable character, such as we Jews delight to let our memory rest upon, to recall the meekness and the charity which fear no betrayal and are never betrayed. And there is, too, his granddaughter, who plays but a small part in this small story, and she sings a song which we take pleasure in quoting for our readers :—

> By the rivers of Babylon, captives, we wept,
>   As a child by its mother forgot ;
> And grief, like an ocean, o'er us swept,
>   For Zion, lov'd Zion, was not !
>
> We hanged our harps on the willow tree boughs,
>   They bid us to sing, but in vain,
> For who, unto song, their hearts can arouse,
>   When bound in Captivity's chain.
>
> Driven like brutes, from strand unto strand,
>   Our minds e'en as fettered as we,
> O give back the land we call our dear land,
>   Where we may still reverence thee !
>
> These climes our loved melodies ne'er shall know,
>   Their words were not writ for the slave,
> For us, hapless Israel, remains but below,
>   Rememb'rance—tears—and the grave !

Of the remaining six stories the last appears by far the best. It treats of the love which "the dark young lord, who, companionless, went his ways, and so wondrous were they that the foolish folk would say that he had learned to commune with the evil one," bore for his brother, "whose tapered hands were meant for naught but to touch the lute and write madrigals for women." The Lord of Falcondale was already a man when this brother was born, yet to his tutor's questioning, "Could'st thou love a brother or a sister?" he could reply, "Aye! with all my soul. More than aught else." He kept his word. Upon that brother he lavished all the absorbing love of a proud absorbed nature. The Lord of Falcondale brought home a wife, and with her came death and destruction. Let the younger lord tell his story as he told it to his instructor:—

You know, father, that ever since I first set mine eyes on my brother's bride, I have avoided her, ay, and him, too. For, according to thy teaching, beloved and honoured instructor, I would not cast mine eyes lovingly on another s treasure, and that other's that of my noble brother. For this reason I have risen earlier than the lark every morning, and have gone away so I should not return till late at night, when all should be in bed. I love the Lady Falcondale as my very soul! Yester-morn, I rose to flee away so early from the castle that the sun had scarce begun to rise when I trod down the stairs. Scarcely, however, had my hand touched the bolt of the gates when I felt my nervous fingers in the iron clasp of someone. Ay, it was my brother! He looked worn and grieved. "Why dost thou fly me thus, my Angelo?" he said in gentle tones, which made me feel doubly, how great a villain I was. "If I have wedded 'tis not because I love thee less, for my love for thee is above the love of woman. What more can I tell thee?" How, after these words, could I tell him the truth? And he said he had been watching my comings and goings, till he could bear no longer. How unworthy his noble love I felt when he grieved over my changed condition. He caught my hands in his, and for the first time in his life I know he wept. Yes, the dark, stern Lord of Falcondale wept silently over me, and said, "My brother, oh, my brother!"

The Lord of Falcondale went away to the Crusades; and during the six years he was away he thought often of his brother. Once he delivered a town from pillage because his eye fell upon one boy who bore a great likeness to his brother. He returned to his castle, he entered by a secret door. His first steps were bent to his brother's chamber, whom he found not. Two cloaks he found in his wife's ante-chamber. Then " words are too feeble to describe that terrible moment. His unerring arm, accustomed to do deadly work, failed not this time."

All the stories have high merit, but the quotations we have given will suffice to convince our readers how readable they are.

"SCOTSMAN," 21st August, 1893.

Seven Stories, by Hélène E. A. Gingold, is a volume of seven short tales of a very fanciful character.

"MANCHESTER EXAMINER," 21st August, 1893.

The *Seven Stories* of Hélène E. A. Gingold are the work of a lady who has won some popularity in poetry, and has now made a departure into the paths of fiction. As a poet Miss Gingold received a certificate of merit from the Duke of Saxe-Coburg Gotha, and as a novelist she seeks the indulgence of the public with somewhat the same feeling that a well-graced actor finds himself before a critical audience in a new part. That, at all events, is the way Miss Gingold puts her own case. I may say that we had not a poet the fewer through this book; only a novelist the more.

"SUNDAY TIMES," August 27th, 1893.

Seven Stories, by Miss Hélène Gingold, has just been published by Messrs. Remington. The authoress, in producing this book, has broken comparatively new ground. Hitherto she has been chiefly known as a poetess of considerable merit, although her other prose works must not be ignored. Her verses have attracted not only the attention of the Press, but also are interesting as having been favourite reading of the late Duke of Saxe-Coburg-Gotha. Miss Hélène Gingold is naturally proud of the commendation of so illustrious a reader, and, in a note at the commencement of her volume, makes the following graceful acknowledgment, referring to some flattering sentiments which had been conveyed to her by the late Duke through his private secretary:

"It is not because they emanate from a royal personage that I value them, but because they are the thoughts of one who has gained a world-wide reputation in the field of art and literature."

The stories, as might be expected from a poetess, are fanciful. Several of them are weird, and all can lay claim to a fair share of originality.

"LEICESTER DAILY POST," 29th August, 1893.

Seven Stories by Hélène E. A. Gingold is a most promising "new departure" by a lady who has already won some thoroughly deserved laurels in the realm of verse. The present series of short tales is nothing if not diversified. One is a story of two religions, another metaphysical, a third an

old-time sporting sketch, the fourth a short story, the fifth
the story of a social problem, while the sixth and seventh
are respectively a true story and a story of the crusades. As
a whole, moreover, their distinguishing fundamental ideas
are clearly conceived and effectively marked out. The
result is that the interest of the reader is speedily aroused
and fully sustained to the close. The new venture of the
authoress, in short, is fully justified by its encouraging
success.

" BELFAST NEWS LETTER," 31st August, 1893.

The authoress, Hélène E. A. Gingold, takes a new
departure in this book. She writes for those persons whose
every hour is precious, and who have little time to spend on
novel reading. Short stories were never in such demand as
the present day, and the writing of good ones is a high art.
Those before us are entitled, "The Rabbi of Moscow" (a
story of two religions); "Veritas" (a metaphysical story);
"How Tom Bellamy won my Lord Hertford's Wager" (an
olden-time sporting story); "Whose was the guilt?" (the
story of a social problem); "The dying Professor" (a true
story); and "The two Brothers" (a story of the Crusades).
The book is well written, and promises to have a wide
circulation.

" NEWCASTLE LEADER," 31st August, 1893.

This is the title of a volume of short stories, which, even
if they had not, as a sort of prefatory letter informs us, received the approbation of the late Duke of Saxe-Coburg-
Gotha, would have had a claim to attention on their own account. The author writes in English, which has occasionally a foreign flavour, but which is, on the whole,
remarkable for its easy grace and its lucidity. The first
of the stories, " The Rabbi of Moscow," is based upon the
the persecution of the Jews in Russia, and although the
period assigned to it is ancient, the motives which enter into
it are avowedly modern. It is a powerful and sympathetic
study—picturesque and imaginative in its treatment of incident, and artistically weird in its presentation of character.
" Veritas," described as a metaphysical story, deserves the

description. The author allows herself the advantage of supernatural machinery, "Veritas" being the spirit of truth, who presents himself to a writer of wayward genius named Mavorel, and who undoubtedly subjects him to strange experiences. It is a mystic but poetic conception. In a different order is "How Tom Bellamy Won my Lord Hertford's Wager," an essay in quaint fiction, which is certainly clever and interesting. These "seven stories" are fresh and original.

"LIVERPOOL MERCURY," 30th August, 1893.

Pleasant reading and fairly-well flavoured with sentiment. There is an attempt at the ideal which Cervantes thought to show in his "Exemplary Novels"; but he found too much human nature for caring to keep to the "Exemplary," and here in "The Ghost Story," "The Metaphysical Story," and such like, there is not the moralising and the rigidity one might expect, but just good, pleasant reading for the young-hearted and for old folk who like to look back.

"THE MORNING," 25th August, 1893.

Messrs. Remington have issued a volume of seven stories by Hélène E. A. Gingold, a favourite author, by the way, of the late Duke of Coburg. They are light and pleasant reading, and one or two of them are something more than interesting.

"THE NEWSAGENT," 26th August, 1893.

Here is another typical volume of tales of the kind we have referred to, and although it is only just to hand we desire to give it a preliminary notice, and hold it over for further review. Miss Hélène E. A. Gingold, previously made her mark with a volume of poems, which was graciously accepted in flattering terms by H.H. the Duke of Saxe-Coburg, who has just passed away, and her former works have been widely appreciated by English and Continental readers. The authoress says in her prefatory notes, "One of my reasons for publishing this volume is that it has appeared to me that short stories are required just as much as long ones. There is many a hard-worked man, aye, and woman too, who, on being asked if they have read this or that novel, answer deprecatingly (of themselves), ' Well, no ; the story is not a short one, and I have not the time.' .... But what of those sons and daughters of earth whose every hour is precious, and who have little time to spend on novel reading ? For these especially I have written my seven short stories, seeing that they are neglected by the rest of writers." Well, they are not all neglected now, but we agree with Miss Gingold, and will turn to her work again. It is beautifully bound in brown cover, gilt lettered, and printed on antique paper, with wide margins.

"THE PEOPLE," 27th August, 1893.

Miss Hélène E. A. Gingold has achieved some reputation as a writer of verse. She now comes before the world as the author of *Seven Stories*, in prose. The stories are short, but many people like short stories better than long ones, and these of Miss Gingold's are fresh and interesting.

" The sensational element is not altogether absent from *Seven Stories.*"—*Saturday Review.*

" There is in them a wealth of earnestness which may succeed in diverting the work-harassed brain."—*National Observer.*

" They are well-written, and will be found exceedingly pleasant reading. They reflect great credit upon the authoress, who is already well known in literary circles."—*Financier.*

"Characterised by variety."—*Glasgow Herald.*

" This bold tale has its characteristic touches ; the strongest at the end. The anti-climax, resulting from the sentence,. ' Sin reigned supreme,' shows the skilful hand and the poetic touch."—*Commerce.*

" Miss Gingold has already written half a dozen successful novels, all of which show wonderful maturity of style."— *Princess.*

" Miss Gingold, the authoress of *Seven Stories*, *Denyse, Steyneville,* and other works, can claim the honour of being one of the youngest writers of to-day and to have written half a dozen works, some of which have passed through as many as six editions."—*Weekly Sun.*

"STEYNEVILLE,"

By Hélène E. A. Gingold.

"SUNDAY TIMES," 9th August, 1885.

"Steyneville," by Hélène E. A. Gingold (Remington), is a clever novel, written in the main extremely well, in imitation of the style in vogue in the time of Queen Anne. This feature is particularly noticeable in the first volume, but less so in the second, and most of all in the third, where the authoress degenerates into decidedly modern English in many and many a page, and this mars an otherwise good book. Then, too, the writing bristles with word anachronisms, such as "cad" and other like expressions, which belong to a later civilisation. The plot of this novel is well conceived and powerfully described; especially is this the case in the tragic scenes, of which there are many. The death of Mr. Steyneville, father of the hero, Harold Steyneville, is exceptionally well told, with much pathos. Most touching is the finding of Almyra Marlande, a young child, lying asleep on the dead body of her kind and generous guardian—a striking contrast—and then her being gently lifted up and carried downstairs by the cold, worldly Lord Alingdale—another striking contrast. What a picture does it not bring before one's eyes! Again worthy of all praise is the love Harold Steyneville bears his dear father when living and when dead the ever-living desire on his part to carefully and well respect the wishes of his deceased parent. What a difference from what is now only too prevalent! want of respect for parents and impatience at all parental control. The character of Almyra, the heroine, is well depicted. She is a beautiful girl, loved by all with whom she comes in contact, but hard, worldly, ambitious, heartless, and vain of her personal attractions. She inflames with love, and throws her lovers aside more thoughtlessly than a pair of gloves; nevertheless, we cannot help liking her, and hoping that her end may be peaceful, the opposite of which is foreshadowed by many expressions. Valerian de Crispigne is a fine character; he is the half-brother and "double" of Harold. His love for his Italian wife and her death are very tragic items. A curious idea is introduced; it is this, that a man, Walter Stanford Hurleham, "the eldest son of the noble house of Carisbrooke," a former lover of Almyra's, enters her husband's service as a valet, and it is on this man that a thrilling part of the narrative turns—the elopement. The likeness of the spy, de la Motte, is well painted, but this character does not deserve much notice. He is useful in the book, however, in several ways. Annie Marlande, though plain, and a great contrast to her beautiful sister, is a very charming girl, and wins our sympathy from the very first. There is too much embracing of one man by another man, too much kissing *coram populo*, and too many tragic speeches to be quite natural, but for all that the book is decidedly above the average of modern fiction, and though the plot is woven in variegated colours, they harmonise and produce no flimsy, worthless article, through which one can see at a glance, but the product is more than usually good, and creates a desire to read to the end, which is very much more than can truly be said of most novels of the present day.

"DAILY TELGRAPH," 18th August, 1885.

By far the most conspicuous literary merit of "Steyneville; or Fated Fortunes" by Hélène E. A. Gingold, is the briskness and vivacity of narrative and dialogue which characterise every part of the three volumes. The story is crowded—perhaps it might be said overcrowded—with incident, and a very considerable number of characters move across the scene, but intricacy of plot is avoided and the interest never flags. Steyneville tells the story of his own life—" the memoirs of an unextraordinary man," they are called—carrying the reader back to the early part of last century, and giving, more or less vividly, a picture of society in those days. The most important personage is Almyra Marlande, a beauty who, after wrecking the happiness of several admirers, marries the Marquis de Sansgêne, whom she ultimately dishonours by an elopement. In her career the heartlessness of frivolous beauty and gaiety is powerfully depicted. Lord Alingdale, Colonel Death, and Lord Stapleton are also well drawn characters. The strong feature, however, of the novel, and that which will probably make it a favourite, is its vigorous action, which sustains the reader's interest and attention throughout, combined with pointed epigrammatic dialogue.

"VANITY FAIR," 7th November, 1885.

This story depends upon characterisation rather than plot. Certain of the incidents are powerful; others are natural and pathetic; but no especial purpose, no complicated story requiring much development runs through the pages. In dealing with people, however, Miss Gingold shows capacity, insight, and a nice discrimination; the characters that she desires we should love are often nobly drawn, while even with the reckless, misguided, and unfortunate heroine we cannot but feel the most keen spmpathy. "Steyneville" is admitted to be only a first attempt. It contains much that places it above the hackneyed productions of more practised lady novelists; and the next effort of the authoress, especially if she departs into a fresh and original field, will be awaited with interest and curiosity.

"MONEY MARKET REVIEW," August 15th, 1885.

As financial journalists, we may be rightly considered to be going far beyond the limits of our proper literary sphere in taking public notice of the productions of the novelist; but in drawing attention to the volumes now before us, we have the less hesitation in going outside our usual functions, firstly, because they are the maiden efforts of a young authoress, and, secondly, because they disclose in almost every page a force of imagination, a subtle insight into character, a culture and grace of style, and power of keeping up a sustained interest in the persons and fortunes of her actors, that warrant a belief that a new writer has come forward who is destined to take a high position in the ranks of the modern school of novelists. It is not our purpose to retell Miss Gingold's story. The service thus rendered is at best an ungrateful one to the author, as to the intending reader, inasmuch as it deprives a perusal of its original charm. The plot is compact in form, and unhampered by a redundancy of subordinate incidents, all of which the authoress keeps in a justly-balanced relation to the principal motive. The characters are drawn with distinctness and precision, and their individualities are preserved from the opening to the finish. Among them is one, Colonel Death, whose fine courage and manly tenderness at once enlist sympathy and make us wish to renew his acquaintance. The heroine Almyra, by turns selfish and self-sacrificing, wayward and firm of purpose, is a clever study, the light and shade of which are, from their depth, in striking contrast with the gentle and even tones that make up the character of her sister Annie. Nor has Miss Gingold failed to draw her hero, Steyneville, in a way to make him throughout an object of pleasant interest. Unity of action, a prime requisite in a good novel, is well maintained in "Steyneville," a story which we have little hesitation in saying will reward the perusal of all who find pleasure in a romance that is free from vulgar, adventitious sensationalism, and is told with an admirable grace and spirit.

"BRITISH AUSTRALASIAN," August 27, 1885.

We have in this novel a first effort by an authoress who has evidently from the text imbibed continental rather than English modes of reasoning, and also occasionally modes of expression. Yet she has chosen a most difficult period for the action of the story, which takes the form of a memoir by a man who, living at the commencement of the last century, rubbed up against Pope and Lady Mary Wortley Montague, and other celebrities of that day. The hero, if we may call Lord Alingdale the hero, is undoubtedly an Atheist; the heroine is altogether a lovely, unloveable creature, and they and the narrator are surrounded by a large concourse of people fast and slow, and the former are free to express themselves, and the latter are allowed to be shocked at what the former say, Taking the time in which the story is supposed to be written into consideration, there are, we think, many expressions used which were then hardly current, but it would give a very false idea of the work if we stopped here. The various characters stand out well upon the page; the action is sustained; there is certainly interest attached to the story, and the writer undoubtedly is at her best in the most difficult situations. There are many portions of the book that rise above the ordinary level; and here are some paragraphs which will serve to show how the writer can express her views:—" I tell thee—young men and boys, profligates and fools, seek the flowers they would wear in hothouses, where false heat hath produced false fragrance and false beauty; wise men and old men, true men and hermits, seek *their* blossoms by the mountain side, where the natural air of Heaven hath made real fragrance and real beauty." Or here again, in describing a man utterly bewitched by the heroine, we read:—" This love, I think, is the most teasing while it lasts, and the most short-lived and ephemeral to boot. . . . . The great art is not to win—that's easy enough—but to keep what is won. Here the whole secret lies. One need not be divinely beautiful or extraordinarily clever to do this, but one must have tact—diplomacy in a man, tact in a woman—a little hypocrisy, and a vast amount of Christian forbearance." We should like to see a second and revised edition.

"LADY," 12th November, 1885.

In a very graceful preface it is admitted that this is a first attempt, but even had it not been so the book would on its merits fairly command attention. The story flows naturally enough, and it has its genuine dramatic episodes and climaxes. As the plot, or rather memoir, advances, so the tone deepens and gathers strength, and even if a certain sadness pervades the chapters, it must be conceded that by adversity, the great nobility of some characters and the lingerind truth and goodness of others, is finally and very naturally made manifest. The authoress depicts perhaps a somewhat over-emotional hero ; but Lord Halifax Allingford, the Colonel, and Almyra are all powerfully drawn and impressive portraits. It is an error perhaps rather than a fault, but the one awkward and inartistic portion of the book is that which deals with the extracts from this or that person's diary. The use of the first person in telling a story offers certain temptations, but, as in the present case, its presents insuperable obstacles when the author is compelled to indicate definitely what is passing in the mind of some person other than the narrator. Hélène Gingold's next effort will be awaited with considerable curiosity.

" MORNING POST," 19th August, 1885.

The author's clever little " Apologue," in which, under the veil of an allegory she tries to foresee the fate that awaits her book, would of itself dispose both reader and critic to indulgence. Her tale is, however, good enough to stand on its own merits. These " memoirs of an unextraordinary man " are full of movement, the action never lags, and there is much variety of incident. The period of the story is that of the last century, naturally, therefore, Jacobinism plays a part, but not a prominent one in it. Many of the characters are graphic portraits, and, despite a certain exaggeration of style, there is much promise in the author's work.

" OBSERVER," January 10th, 1886.

Alike in subject and in treatment, Miss Gingold's novel departs with successful boldness from the beaten paths of young ladies' romance. Its style is thoroughly fresh, if occasionally somewhat incorrect ; much care has been taken to suggest the tone of the period—the reign of Queen Anne—in which the scene of the action is laid, and the character-drawing, though fanciful, and sometimes exaggerated, has plenty of spirit and individuality.

The hero of " Steyneville," described in its title page as an "unextraordinary man," is brought up as page-in-waiting to the Lady Olympia Norton, a post which he obtains through the patronage of Halifax Lord Alingdale, a notorious gallant of the day. His story is told in the form of an autobiography, interspersed here and there with quotations from the diaries of other people, and especially from that kept by his pretty cousin, Almyra Marlande. Almyra is a terrible flirt from her childhood upwards, and she gives Harold Steyneville, who is left her guardian, all sorts of trouble. In the first place her beauty leads him to fall head over ears in love with her, he in his turn being the object of her less attractive sister's devotion· Almyra, on her side, never seriously regards her worthy but somewhat priggish cousin as a lover, but goes heart-whole on her way, trying to turn the head of every man she comes across. One of her many admirers is that same Lord Alingdale who gave Harold Steyneville his first start in life, and a very undesirable match his lordship seems for any self-respecting young woman. Lord Alingdale is introduced to the reader in a passage intended, no doubt, to explain the strong influence which he exerts over the character of the writer.

"Amongst our visitors of note was a certain Lord Halifax Alingdale—handsome, opulent and young. Possessing these advantages, one would have supposed an ordinary man to be content with his lot; but my lord was not. Impatient and restless, he had already from early youth plunged into the wildest excesses and debaucheries; and now almost tired of every pleasure that life and wealth could give, he cursed his fate incessantly. My father, indeed, was the only person whose counsel made any impression on him.. He believed in nothing, and sneered at everything and everybody—himself most of all. As he plays an important part in this history, I will endeavour to describe his person.

"In stature, he was tall and lithe. His countenance was at once striking and repelling ; being perfectly clean shaven, his finely-chiselled features were clear and handsome as a cameo's. His eyes, of some dark, nameless hue, more elongated than wide, and rather deeply sunk into his head, were surrounded by long black eyebrows. His mouth was exceptionally small, indeed, almost effeminate, but for the strange expression it invariably wore. The corners were curved upwards into a half-smile, inexpressibly bitter and dark. His fine chesnut-coloured hair fell in natural curls over his shoulders ; although Mr. Harley, or St. John, I forget which, had made ribands very modish, my lord preferred, though in every other way fastidious in his dress, to be old-fashioned in this one particular style. Although always habited with neatness and excellent taste, rather than be considered a coxcomb or a fop,. I think he would have sooner erred the other way. His tolerance and utter indifference passed for good humour ; so that he was extremely popular with almost all. His conversation was mostly clever, though often caustic and bitter. His sarcasm, indeed, could be so barbed and pointed that his enemies—and he had many—scarcely cared to come within the range of his poisoned shafts."

When a man's eyes are of a "dark, nameless hue," he is generally one of the heroes of a lady novelist, and in other respects Lord Alingdale is typical of his tribe. Years of vicious excess fail to cause any serious degeneration of his nature if one is to judge by his recorded acts, and not by his conversation. A blatant atheist, a selfish voluptuary, and a man given over to reckless excess of every kind, Lord Alingdale is yet represented as behaving at every crisis of the story like a gallant gentleman, not only without fear, but without reproach. He is just the kind of extraordinary character that we should expect to fascinate a girl like Almyra Marlande, especially if she had drunk deep of the romance of her day ; and, indeed, he is so delightfully wicked that if Mistress Marlande's pride had allowed it she would readily become his wife. But she takes it into her pretty head that she is being wooed out of pity, and that his lordship is not quite in earnest in his protestations ; so in spite of the doubtful advice of her relations and friends she declines to become Lady Alingdale, and becomes the Marquise de Sansgêne instead. From this elderly husband she runs away with " the eldest son of the house of Carisbrooke," who in order to be near her has entered her service as a footman. In her flight she is pursued by not only her faithful kinsman, Steyneville, but by her rejected suitor, Alingdale, and by his honest ally, Colonel Death. How and where she is found, the manner of her repentance, and the effect of her death in effecting Alingdale's reformation—these things are romantically told and supply the main plot of the novel.

"HERTS GUARDIAN," 8th September, 1885.

The authoress of this novel is a new aspirant to literary fame, which she bids fair to attain. The period of action is laid during the early part of the last century. The language is for the most part appropriate to the period—we say advisedly for the most part, as here and there the characters use expressions quite unknown during the Georgian era. To give even an outline of the somewhat intricate plot would be a difficult task—indeed it would be unfair to the reader to indicate how the final *denouement* is brought about. Suffice it to say that the tangled skein is unwound with singular skill. There is an individuality in the characters which is rarely met with in modern novels. The *rôle* of the hero, Harold Steyneville, is really subservient to that of Almyra, a haughty, heartless, self-willed beauty ; this character is powerfully drawn ; although she is by no means all bad, she fails to obtain the sympathy of the reader, though interest in her fortunes is unflaggingly maintained. Annie, Almyra's sister, is an excellent foil to the impetuous heroine. Each and every of the other personages is delineated with breadth and vigour by a masterly hand. In *Steyneville*, Miss Gingold not only affords evidence of originality of ideas and keen perception of character, but also of her ability of describing her thoughts in clear and forcible language.

WHITEHALL REVIEW, August 6th, 1886,

The story runs very evenly, and the author's style is a particularly good one.

"JEWISH WORLD," September 25th, 1885.

The evidence of skill, power, and imagination, promises ultimately to secure for the writer a first rank amongst the sisterhood of novelists.

"A CYCLE OF VERSE,"
By Helene E. A. Gingold.

"NEW YORK HERALD," April 8, 1889.

This is a neat, carefully-printed volume of poetry, evidently from the pen of a young woman of accomplishments and feeling. In a preface we are informed that many of the poems were written in youth, some before the age of fifteen. In this respect Miss Gingold recalls Lord Byron; and in another respect likewise, as she dedicates her volume to his memory, as indicative of her " deepest admiration and humblest respect." We might expect from this inspiration a Byronic influence, as most young writers are apt to follow his lordship in communing with despair and dark imaginings. Miss Gingold does not permit admiration to become imitation. Her poetic style shows no trace of the Giaours or the Laras; but, on the contrary, is clear, direct, and true—altogether her own. Here, for instance, where a simple thought is told, as in a sonnet, with the simplicity of Wordsworth:

> There are two books I love to read,
> So fair are they, so deep indeed,
> And strangely true, that when I dare
> View from 'neath their covers fair
> What to me is plain by writ,
> I feel unworthy, little fit,
> To be the one to recognise
> The mystic lore that in them lies
> I—of all! For never a sage
> Of these dear works could solve a page,
> Or guess their aim, or ever tell,
> As I—one-hundredth part as well—
> The boundless love and trust that lies
> In those two books—my dearest's eyes.

Miss Gingold's distinguishing trait is sincerity. The tendency of most modern verse, especially under the influence of Mr. Swinburne, has been to submerge sense and sentiment in a confusion of sounds. And as no one since Shelley has been so completely the master of rhythm as Swinburne, the reader is constantly troubled to know what he means. To euphony Miss Gingold apparently gives negative or relative consideration. It is not the form of saying it, but what she has to say. Carlyle was wont to regard this as an objection to poetry in general, holding that if anybody had a message for the world he should say it and not sing it.

This, however, is only partly true, like much of Mr. Carlyle's philosophy. The spirit of poetry will be found in euphony and form. And if Miss Gingold continues in her poetic career with the promise which these admirable verses show, she will learn that the masters were those who study the melody of the tongue. There are lines in Virgil which, as mere sounds, have a meaning to those who do not know Latin. Lord Tennyson, like Mr. Browning, has put aside form whenever it took his fancy, and said the rudest things in the crudest way; but no writer has ever so refined again and again until his verses ring and sing. A startling thought from Mr. Browning will fall upon the reader like an aerolite, with no regard to prosody or even grammar, and in its deep meaning we forget its lawlessness. But the same thought could have come from Shakespeare like the music of the spheres or the infinite harmonies of the forest and the sea.

Miss Gingold will find, if she pursues her work in this spirit, that there are mysteries in this noble English tongue which will well repay the labour of those who search. It must be labour however, of those who seek for the diamond and quartz, working through clay and sand to the perfect beauty within. The blending of the feeling, sentiment, high thoughts, and womanly aspirations which pervade her writings, with the harmony of sound which belongs to true poetry, should give us a work in time which will hold no mean place in the literature of England.

Miss Gingold acknowledges in some weighty lines her indebtedness to Congreve, and, indeed, her principal poem, "Belcanto," is spoken of as an imperfect tribute to Congreve's memory. Here are four lines called "An Answer," which Congreve might have written:

> Oh, call me what thou wilt, dear fair,
> I all to thee resign;
> God or fiend—I do not care,
> So but you call me *thine* !

Here are other lines which might have been written in the seventeenth century:

TEMPORI PARENDUM.

> Oh, I have read of golden days,
> In times that speak in mortals' praise,
> That truth once in the land did dwell,
> And ladies loved both long and well;

And knights were led—ah, blessed clime
Had I existed in that time
I would have lived to love, I vow,
And not have loved to live—like now!
Oh, I have read of later age—
In history's unromantic page—
That ladies' love endures not long,
The truth is weak, and scorn is strong.
So for constant love and for courtly ways,
Give me the life in those olden days.

In some respects the " Ballade of Belle," an imitation of a poem in the Percy collection, is the best in the volume. The spirit of the old ballad is maintained, and the stories told with the quaintness of Chaucer.

How far Miss Gingold will confine her manifest gifts to poetry it would be rash to assume in so young a writer. Poetry is generally the overture to serious work in literature, as was seen in the writings of Scott, Swift, and Addison. Whether she continues to invoke the Muses or seeks the humble and more expansive method of prose for whatever message she may have for the world, we may safely congratulate her from the promise contained in this volume upon a notable and useful career.

" THE DAILY TELEGRAPH," 27th June, 1889.

Apparently a keen appreciation of Lord Byron's poems and a lively fancy are responsible for Miss Hélène E. A Gingold's modest volume, "A Cycle of Verse" (Remington). Here is a young poetess who felt herself touched by the divine fire at a very early age, and we must believe, without seeking the advice or guidance of some experienced friends, plunged at once into the dangerous intoxication of poetry. At fifteen she was grappling with subjects which a poet of four times the experience would have approached with hesitation, and at twenty she seems to have been sighing, like Alexander, for more poetic worlds to conquer. Miss Gingold, if we may judge by her portrait at the commencement of the booklet, is still young, and what is also hopeful is that her verses appear to improve in the order of their chronological sequence. It would have been better if she had not put her earliest efforts so prominently forward, but in many of the lines which come after these there is much poetic feeling, and an easily recognisable appreciation—the safest ground-work for a young ambition—of some of our master bards.

"QUEEN," 1st JUNE, 1889.

To this volume is prefixed a portrait of the author, from which we infer that she is still young and fair, but she tells us in her preface that some of these pieces were written before she was fifteen. It is apparent that her genius was precocious, and that while pursuing her early studies she exercised herself in writing verse, This collection is more gay and lively than grave and solemn, and many of the pieces are slight and fanciful. At the same time we find interpersed among the rest some which are well considered and thoughtful as a whole, they will afford pleasant reading to those who like new poetry. Moreover, the volume is quite nicely got up.

"SUNDAY TIMES," MAY 1889.

This very interesting little volume, which is embellished with a portrait of the fair author peeping through a lyre, is a kind of literary survival.

"SHEFFIELD TELEGRAPH," 22nd August, 1889.

"A CYCLE OF VERSE," by Hélène E. A. Gingold, has reached a second edition within a very short time of its publication, a great success to be obtained by what is practically the author's début in verse. When the authoress informs us that many of the verses were written before the age of 15, we are prepared to make every allowance, "on the tender ground of extreme youth," yet a perusal of the verses shows that they need no such excuse.

"CORK EXAMINER," 14th June, 1889.

If we were to be asked what was the special feature in this volume which is calculated to arrest attention and cause it to be singled out from rivals, we should be inclined to say its unconventionality. The writer is evidently young, and if we may judge from the portrait prefixed, is also fair; and it would seem to us as if in her poetry she took, not only the poet's license, but the license which is accorded everywhere to a pretty woman. She pours out her thoughts and feelings with a spontaneity which makes itself felt, and which exercises a charm of its own upon the reader. Her moods are varied, grave and gay, lively, and often very severe. Some of her poems have touches of that airy, delicate satire we associate with Praed; now and then we come upon one of those surprising turns which remind us of Heine. The poem " Belcanto " is a striking picture of the sentimental egotist, the singer who enchains the female heart while his own remains dull to any consideration but that of what " pays ; " and it is in the very best manner of society verses. A pathetic German story is very movingly told, and in musical accents, in " The Wanderer's Farewell." Its apostrophes to the Rhine are very effective even in ears which have been familiar with the thousand strains in which the majestic flood has been sung. There is passion mingled with that painful humour of the German poet in the following, addressed to " Madelon of Smyrna : "

> Whene'er thou wear'st thy mirthful mien,
>   I say thou art bright laughter's queen ;
> When from thy lids the teardrops flow,
>   I say that thine's the height of woe ;
> When anger flashes from thine eyes,
>   'Tis fierce as lightning in the skies ;
> And when thou tun'st thy lute to sing,
>   Methinks I hear the lark on wing.
> But when thou say'st in accents low,
>   " My heart's sole light I love thee so,"
> That phrase so short, those words so brief,
>   Make me weep in bitter grief.

It is but turning a page and we find the writer thus capable of being melted rising into the fiercest scorn and denouncing cynicism with all the eloquent intolerance of youth and enthusiasm. Throughout the volume this characteristic of variety runs, and the reader is carried, a willing captive, through pretty love songs, melodious narrative, stinging epigram, and pleasant satire. The little book is full of interest, and can scarcely fail to reach a wide popularity.

" FOLKESTONE OBSERVER," 27th July, 1889.

A dainty little volume, happily named " A Cycle of Verse." The authoress is young, and, what is of more importance, talented. The verses are bright, cleverly written, and redolent of true rhythm. Miss Gingold appears to have taken Spencer and Chaucer as models of style and metre, and has boldly, and, we may add, successfully worked on original lines of her own. Particularly good are the " Lines to my Nephew " and " To Idylline." The " Cycle " has passed into a third edition, and this fact speaks for itself. We understand that Miss Gingold has in hand a sensational novel, which will shortly be published.

"FOLKESTONE JOURNAL," 31st July, 1889.

"A CYCLE OF VERSE," demands special notice on several grounds. The poetry is by Miss Héléne Gingold, a young lady whose portrait, fittingly framed in a lyre, forms the frontispiece. From this portrait it is evident that Nature has been kind to the young authoress both with respect to mental and physical gifts.

"THE JEWISH WORLD," 26th April, 1889.

"A CYCLE OF VERSE." This is the title of a dainty little volume of poems which has just been published by Messrs. Remington & Co., and of which Miss Héléne Gingold is the author. Miss Gingold is already favourably known by her novels ; and her reputation can only be enhanced by these musical efforts in verse, although many of them were written before the age of fifteen. The range of subjects and style is exceedingly wide for so youthful a writer. "The Hebrew Maiden's Lament " is a passionate embodiment of the genius of Jewish History, while in the " Ballade of Belle " the quaint spirit of the old Percy ballads is caught with hardly less truth. Miss Gingold's poetical genius seems, however, to have been principally nourished by Congreve and the writers of his time. Her opening poem, " Belcanto," is intended as a tribute to this dominating influence, traces of which may be detected throughout her volume. Miss Gingold shows undeniable poetic gifts, which it is to be hoped she will assiduously cultivate. A career of no small distinction is open to her if she fulfils the promise of her first " Cycle of Verse."

"LADY," 12th November, 1889.

"A CYCLE OF VERSE, by Hélène E. A. Gingold.—In the preface to her prettily got up work, the writer says that she wrote many of the poems therein contained at a very early age, "at a time when the heart is unsubdued by the weight of years, responsibility, and sorrowful experience." We detect youth in many of the lines, which lack the cunning of construction, which age and experience brings. But none the ess welcome do we find them.

Pocos meses hace llegó á nuestras manos un elegante libro, así titulado: "*A Cycle of Verse*," *by Helene E. A. Gingold, Author of 'Steyneville,' 'Denyse,'* " etc.: era una colección de poesías inglesas, dedicada "á la memoria de lord Byron, aquel luminar de la literatura británica," y leyendo el índice, observamos que algunas composiciones tenían por título un nombre español, como *Angelay Benita*; pertenecía á la segunda edición (porque la primera fué agotada en breves días), y figuraban al final de la obra, según práctica editorial en el extranjero, los diversos juicios críticos del libro publicados por numerosos periódicos de Inglaterra, Francia, Italia, Grecia y por nuestro distinguido colega *La Epoca*, de Madrid.

Uno de esos juicios es debido al afamado crítico sir Edwin Arnold, en *The Daily Telegraph*, y termina de este modo: "Parece que miss Hélène Gingold aspira á los veinte años, cual otro Alejandro, á conquistar nuevos mundos para la poesía."

Miss Elena Gingold, cuyo retrato publicamos en la pág. 84, nació en Londres el 17 de Marzo de 1867, y tiene, por consiguiente, la edad dé veintitrés años, aun no cumplidos; sus padres, ricos negociantes de la City, la dieron esmerada educación, en consonancia con sus aptitudes, pudiendo sin ascrúpulos dedicarla, á los doce años, al estudio de los autores clásicos de Inglaterra, Grecia y Francia; á los diez siete años, miss Elena publicó sn primera novela, intitulada *Steyneville*, y la crítica, al ocuparse en ella, teniendo en cuenta la temprana edad de la autora, y tolerando ciertas audacias prosódicas que censuraron los puristas, incluyó el nombre de miss Gingold en la lista de los buenos novelistas ingleses, llegando á decir un periódico (que no brilla por su indulgencia), al dar cuenta de la aparición de *Steyneville*: "Es simplemente maravilloso que una niña haya escrito novela tan notable."

A esta obra siguió *Denyse*, novela más pensada y mejor conducida que la primera, pero no menos moral ni más ingenua, y al éxito extraordinario que obtuvo debió su joven autora que editores importantes de ambos continentes solicitaran su colaboración en revistas de arte, ciencias y literatura; y los trabajos de esta naturaleza que miss Gingold ha dado á la estampa durante dos años son muestra evidente á más de su inspiración y su talento, de su pasmosa laboriosidad.

Cuando el público y los editores esperaban una tercera

novela que consolidase el título de distinguida novelista que tan fácilmente había conquistado, miss Gingold sorprendió á unos y otros revelándose poetisa de gran vuelo con la pnblicación de su libro *A Cycle of Verse*, obra muy severamente analizada por la crítica, y en la cual su autora sigue las huellas de lord Byron; las dos primeras ediciones fueron agotadas en pocos meses y la tercera, recientemente publicada, está ya en vías de tener igual afortunada suerte que las anteriores.

Si el tiempo no malogra la esperanza que han hecho concebir las críticas severas y las entusiastas alabanzas dedicadas á las obras de miss Gingold, la dormida poesía inglesa deberá su resurrección al purísimo aliento de una niña, dotada por Dios de los bellos encantos de la mujer y de la audaz concepción de un inspiradísimo vate.

"EVENING NEWS," April 5th, 1889.

Miss Hélène Gingold, who is known to the public as the author of "Steyneville" and "Denyse," now appears as a poetess with her lyre on the frontispiece of "A Cycle of Verse," which shows marvellous versatility of style. "To Idylline" is tenderly gay. "The Greatest Books" is deeply passionate. "Thoughts to a Patriot Friend" are philosophic beyond the seeming of the fair girlish face in the portrait. On the other hand, "O Lady, ask not," is pathos itself. In a different vein could anything be better than Miss Gingold's description of cramming for an examination in "The Land of Learning?"

Hamm'ring as the hours sped
(They never slept, but read and read)
In their minds, like countless tin-tacks,
Dates of wars, and rules of syntax.

The author ranges over the whole gamut of the emotions, besides touching on many a topic of light laughter, which throws into the better relief the artistic despondency of the little poem called "When," which would most musically wed itself to some tender theme for piano or guitar.

"BIRMINGHAM DAILY GAZETTE," April 22nd, 1889.

Her songs are really songs that suggest their own music, and there is an undercurrent of real passionate feeling in such pieces as "When," "To a Withered Flower," &c. In the narrative poems the author displays the requisite talent of being simple and concise. The best of the pieces of this class is probably her rendering in verse of the "Legend of Die Frauenkirche, Munich."

"LIFE," April 18th, 1889.

Young and beautiful, endowed with a poetic spirit and appreciation, Miss Hélène Gingold appeals to the public for gentle judgment on her verse, much of which was written at a very early age.

Earnestness of thought and feeling are distinctly present in Miss Gingold's poems, and in the present volume there is so much promise that there is every reason to believe that in future we shall hear more of the author of "A Cycle of Verse."

"FOLKESTONE NEWS," 27th July, 1889.

We have just received from Messrs. Remington & Co., a book of poems, entitled "A Cycle of Verse," by Hélène A. Gingold. This lady is already known as the author of "Steyneville" and "Denyse," and this her latest venture will, we feel sure, serve to considerably increase her reputation. The portrait of Miss Gingold on the frontispiece would of itself give one the idea that she was a person endowed with rare poetic feeling, and a perusal of the volume (very beautifully got up, by the way) would afford abundant evidence that she is gifted with great powers of expression. When we say that some of the poems were written at a very early age it will account for one or two slight blemishes; but further research shows that as she has advanced in age her poetical powers have become more fully developed. We would draw particular attention to "Ages Ago," "Thoughts to a Patriot Friend," and "The Greatest Books." Some of the songs, too, are very pretty, and set to music would, we doubt not, in a short time be in great favour with vocalists. "A Cycle of Verse" will be sure to meet with a good deal of appreciation from a large circle of readers. The volume has already reached a second edition, and the third will shortly be issued.

"THE SEASON," August, 1889.

There has lately been published by Remington and Co., under the title of "A Cycle of Verse," a graceful little collection of poems by Hélène Gingold, already known as the author of "Steyneville" snd "Denyse." Owing to a diversity in their period of production (some having been written before the age of fifteen), the poems differ widely in merit, but many amongst them show marked poetic talent, sufficiently strong to encourage future efforts. Conspicuously charming amongst the varied selection are "The Land of Learning," "To a Withered Flower," and the quaint original lines, headed "The Greatest Books."

"IL POPOLO ROMAN," 23rd September, 1890.

E' un elegantissimo volume di poesie inglesi, assai pregevoli. L' autrice, imita qua e là felice—mente la causticità byroniana, ed il suo verso è armonioso e lo stile chiaro e piano. La Signora Gingold, che non è alla sua prima prova, essendo favorevolmente conosciuta per altri lavori letterari, ha qualità rare di poetessa e l' accoglienza fatta dal pubblico a questi suoi versi, che sono già arrivati alla terza edizione, lo dimostra.

"LA PERSEVERANZA di GIOVEDI MILANO,"
1st August, 1889.

Questo elegante volumetto *doré sur tranche* contiene una raccolta di poesi che non mancano di pregi. L' autrice s' è nutrita di Byron e talvolta ne imita felicemente il tono caustico e satirico. Non v' è grande pretesa d'invenzione, ma il verso è armonioso, lo stile chiaro e piano ; vi si vorrebbe però trovare più di quella qualità che gli inglesi chiamano *raciness*, ossia robustezza e sapore piccante. Nella prefazione la Signora Gingold (che non è nuova alla letterautra, avendo già pubblicato altri lavori d'imaginazione) chiede venia della sua audacia nell' esporsi al pubblico come poetessa. Le si può rispondere con l' *Alceste* di Molière :

Quel besoin si pressant avez-vous de rimer ?
Et qui diantre vous pousse à vous fair imprimer ?

Veramente la Signora Gingold può aspettarsi dal pubblico un giudizio più favorevole di quello proferito dal misantropo di Molière, poichè, ripetiamo, i suoi versi hanno pregi reali non comuni.

"LA EPOCA," 10th August, 1889.

Asi modestamente se intitula un tomo de poestas publicado por los editores Remington Remington and Ca., de Londres.

Su autor, mis Helena E. A. Gingold, muy conocida en la república de las letras por sus novelas *Steyneville*, *Denyse* y otras de un valor literario indiscutible, dice en el prológo que muchas de las composiciones poéticas que da al público las compuso cuando apenas contaba quince años. Leidas éstas, si no se tratara de miss Gingold, cuya ingenua sinceridaa supera tan sólo su hermosura, podría el lector muy bien dispensarse de creer que una niña de quince años, sid experiencia del mundo, sin pesadumbres, sin pasiones, puenp haber escrito poesias de tan levantado vuelo.

A Byron dedica miss Gingold sus versos, y á fe que si no

imita al gran poeta, le sigue bien de cerca y le alcanza algunas veces.

La primera composición que presenta el libro, titulada *Belcanto*, basta ella sola para revelar un poeta de primera fuerza. Ternura, vigor, atrevidas concepciones ante las cuales un hombre vacilara, imágenes verdaderamente esculturales, profundos conceptos fiilosóficos, sentimiento, idealismo, nobles vías, amor de todo lo bello y grande que el poeta sueña en sus dulces horas de apacible inspiración, encierra en sus paginas el libro *A Cycle of Verse*.

Fortuna y grande ha sido para la decadente poesía inglesa que miss Helena E. A. Gingold se haya decidido á dar á la publicidad con sus conposiciones de niña sus concepciones de mujer. El favor, inusitado en esta clase de obras, que el público ha despensado al libro que nos ocupa servirá quizás de fecundo estímulo para que otros desconocidos ú olvidados poetas, que han trocado el arpa por la árida pluma del periodista ó por el escudriñador escalpelo de la novela, vuelvan de nuevo al palenque á probar fortuna Miss Gingold les ha dado el grito de alerta: dudamos que la alcancen, pero en seguir sus huellas habrá gloria bastante para no desesperar de que vuelva á ser la poesía la inseparable compañera del *home* en Inglaterra.

" LA EPOCA," 20th February, 1890

El último número de *La Illustración Espanola y Americana* ofrece un testimonio más de que tan importante publicación es una verdadera y completísima crónica illustrada, é ilustrada por varios conceptos, de la vida española y de la de Madrid principalmente.

En el texto figuran notables trabajos que llevan las firmas de los Sres. Fernández Bremón, Conde de Coello, Fontaura y Monreal, y entre los grabados los retratos del nuevo Ministro de Fomento, Sr. Duque de Veragua, del illustre é inolvidable Conde de Toreno, y del veterano actor Mariano Fernández; las reproducciones de un lindo cuadro de Díaz Carreño, " El primer desengaño," y de un precioso dibujo de Alcázar, " Al baile," y ostros representando el interior del nuevo local del Círculo de *Bellas Artes*; el último responso ante el cadáver del Conde de Toreno, y los pabellones construídos en el Observatorio de San Fernando para las operaciones astro fotograficas, en virtud de las cuales se proponen hoy los hombres de ciencia levantar el plano del cielo.

Por circunstancias especiales descuellan en el mismo número la continuación de la obra *En Marruecos*, recuerdos de viaje, una de las producciones más hermosas de Pierre Lotį (Luis Mariá Julian Viau), el célebre autor de *Pêcheur de Islande*, y el retrato de una joven poetisa inglesa, miss Elena E. A. Gingold, que es muy notable como artista y bellísima como mujer.

Miss Gingold, hija de unos ricos negociantes de la *City*, en Londres, que apenas cuenta veinte años, es autora de dos novelas, *Steyneville y Denysse*, y de un tomo de poesias, *A Cycle of Verse*, que le han conquistado en su país grande y verdadera celebridad.

"LE COURIER DE LONDRES ET DE L'EUROPE,"
21st April, 1889.

LES LIVRES EN ANGLETERRE.

La librairie Remington & Co. vient de publier un recueil de poésies auquel on peut prédire dès aujourd'hui le plus legitime succès. Le livre est d'une débutante, il est vrai, car Miss Helene Gingold, son auteur, offre aujourd'hui au public ses premières poésies, dont plusieurs—dit la préface—furent composées alors qu'elle n'avait point encore 15 ans.

Miss Gingold rappelle par plus d'un côte Lord Byron, à la mémoire de qui elle dédie son œuvre. Pourtant, si elle l'admire, elle ne l'imite pas servilement. Sa langue est claire, simple et frappée au coin du naturel et de la sincérité.

Miss Gingold, en effet, ne tombe point comme Shelley et Swinburne dans la recherche exagérée du rhytmé et ne s'attache pas seulement à faire des vers harmonieux ou cadencés. Elle se souvient du reproche que Carlyle faisait à la poésie et de ce mot du philosophe : " Si vous avez quelque chose à dire, dites-le, mais ne le chantez pas."

Bien que cette opinion ne soit exacte qu'à moitie, it faut savoir gré à Miss Gingold d'avoir exprimé de très belles idées en beaux vers et d'avoir joint ici, selon un dicton populaire, l'utile a l'agréable.

Qu'elle cherche encore, qu'elle poursuive son œuvre, et elle trouvera que la langue qu'ella manie si bien possède des trésors ignorés, dont la découverte la récompensera de ses peines. Elle arrivera ainsi à réunir les " vastes pensées," la délicatesse de sentiment, les aspirations élevées qui remplissent son œuvre à l'harmonie de la forme, et créera ainsi une œuvre qui occupera bientôt une place importante dans la literature anglaise.

Nous voudrions citer tout au long quelques-uns de ces jolis poémes quelques-uns de ces vers charmants que l'on rencontre a chaque page du livre. La place nous manque malheureusment, et nous devons nous borner à signaler au lecture le poéme principal, " Belcanto," que Congreve n'aurait pas désavoue ; la ballade de la " Belle," naïve et simple comme un chant de Chaucer.

Miss Helene Gingold a passé plusieurs années à Paris ; elle y compte de nombreux amis dans les lettres et les arts, et nous sommes heureux de pouvoir lui apporter—à elle qui sait si bien apprécier notre littérature—notre modeste part d'éloges et de félicitations.

" LE TELEPHONE," 1st July, 1889.

C'est du Nord aujourd'hui que nous vient la lumière.

Autrement dit, nous recevons d'Angleterre un recueil de poésies, publié par la librairie Remington et Cie à Londres, qui nous paraît appelé au plus grand succès, s'il procure au public la dixième partie du plaisir que nous avons éprouvé à sa lecture.

L'auteur, Mlle. Hélène Gingold, est une débutante, croyons-nous, et plusieurs de ses poésies ont été composées, nou dit la préface, alors qu'elle avait à peine quinze ans. On ne s'en douterait nullement : ces poésies ont en effet toute la fraîcheur et la naïveté de la jeunesse, mais ne trahissent pas l'inexpérience du début ; la langue en est claire, simple, et surtout pleine de naturel et de simplicité.

Nous voudrions citer tout au long quelques-uns de ces jolis poèmes, de ces vers charmants que l'on rencontre à chaque page, et qui ne permettent de déposer livre qu'après l'avoir achevé. Mais nous devons nous borner à signaler au passage à nos lecteurs quelques poésies : *Idyline*, d'une douce et tendre gaîté, *Oh ! ne demandes pas, La Complainte, La Vie et la mort, Lamentation, Homo homini lupus, Une réponse, Belcantô*, et la ballade *de la Belle*, naïve et simple comme un chant de Chaucer.

Mlle. Hélène Gingold a passé plusieurs années à Paris, où elle a laissé de nombreux amis dans les arts et dans les lettres ; son livre rencontrera, non seulement auprès d'eux, mais auprès du public, le plus sympathique accueil, le plus légitime succés.

ΕΠΙΘΕΩΡΗΣΙΣ.

A Cycle of Verse. By Hélène A. Gingold. (London Remington and Co.)

Ἐκ Λονδίνου ἐστάλησαν ἡμῖν ἐν λαμπρᾷ ἐκδόσει χαριέστατα καὶ ὑψιπετῆ ποιήματα τῆς κυρίας Hélène Gingold ὑπὸ τὸν ἀνωτέρω τίτλον. Ἀναγνόντες αὐτὰ κατεγοητεύθημεν· ἐὰν δὲ κρίνωμεν ἐκ τῆς ἐν ἀρχῇ εἰκόνος τῆς ποιητρίας, ὁ ἀγγλικὸς Παρνασσὸς ἀπέκτησε μίαν περιπλέον ὡραίαν Ἀμαδρυάδα ἐν ταῖς δροσώδεσι καὶ ἀειθαλέσιν αὐτοῦ λόχμαις. Ὡς ἡ ἀρχαία ἡμῶν φιλολογία, οὕτω καὶ ἡ ἀγγλικὴ δὲν στερεῖται τῶν Σαπφῶν της. Ἴσως ἡ μόνη ὡραία τέχνη, ἣν μετὰ χάριτος (ἐξιδιασμένον τοῦτο προτέρημα τοῦ ὡραίου φύλου) καλλιεργοῦσι γυναῖκες εἶναι ἡ ποίησις· ἀφοῦ εἰς τὴν μουσικήν. εἰς ἣν πλεῖσται νεάνιδες ἐκπαιδεύονται, οὐδὲν ἄξιον λόγου παρήγαγον ἐν συγκρίσει πρὸς τὸ τραχύτερον φῦλον.

Ἐν τοῖς ποιήμασι τῆς κυρίας Gingold πανταχοῦ διαφαίνεται καταθέλγουσα χάρις, καίτοι τὸ εἶδος τῆς ποιήσεως δὲν εἶναι πανταχοῦ Σαπφικόν.

Πολλαχοῦ διαβλέπομεν τὴν Βυρώνειον σχολήν, ἀλλαχοῦ ἀναμιμνησκόμεθα τῶν ἡμετέρων Γνωμικῶν ποιητῶν· καίτοι τὸ Old Poet καὶ Frauenkirche ἴσως θὰ ἦσαν περισσότερον at home ὑπὸ γερμανικὸν γλωσσικὸν ἔνδυμα.

Βαθεῖαι φιλοσοφικαὶ παρατηρήσεις ὡς τιμαλφεῖς λίθοι κεῖνται οἱονεὶ ἐγκατεσπαρμένοι ἐπὶ διαχρύσου δαπέδου. Ἡ ἀποστροφὴ To a Cynic περιέχει βαθυτάτην φιλοσοφικὴν ἀλήθειαν. Τοῦτο δὲ τοσούτῳ μᾶλλον μᾶς ἐκπλήττει, καθόσον ὁ φιλοσοφικὸς οὗτος ποιητὴς οὔτε ῥυτίδας ἔχει οὔτε μαρασματώδεις παρειάς, ἀλλὰ κατὰ τὸ Σοφόκλειον ἐκεῖνο " ἐν μαλακαῖς παρειαῖς νεάνιδος ἐννηχεύει τοιοῦτον φιλοσοφικὸν πνεῦμα."

Προωρισμένη ὅπως καταστῇ ἡ ἰδία ἀντικείμενον ᾀσμάτων, ἡ Gingold προυτίμησεν αὐτὴ νὰ ψάλλῃ· τὸ δὲ ἀνθεμόεν ποιητικὸν στέμμα, ὅπερ τοσοῦτον εὐπρεπῶς ἐπικοσμεῖ τὴν πλήρη ποιήσεως εἰκόνα αὐτῆς, πρέπει νὰ ὁμολογήσωμεν, ὅτι ἐπαξίως θὰ τῇ ἐπεδικάζετο καὶ ὑπὸ τοῦ πλέον αὐστηροῦ ὁμίλου ἑλλανοδικῶν.

Δ.

(*Translation.*)
SPECTATOR, ATHENS, Oct., 1889.

───◆───

A very handsome little book of graceful and ambitious poetry bearing the above title has been sent to us from London. We have been greatly charmed by its perusal, and if one may judge from the portrait of the authoress, prefixed to the volume, the English Parnassus can boast of at least one more fair Hamadryad in its dewy evergreen thickets. In English, as well as in our own ancient literature, Sapphos have flourished and still flourish. The art of poetry is perhaps the only fine art cultivated successfully, and with peculiar grace (that special appanage of the fair sex), by women; for in music, although it is almost universally studied by them, they have produced nothing to rival the work of the stronger sex. In Miss Gingold's work there is everywhere noticeable a most enchanting grace of manner, although her poetry is not all of the Sapphic school. In places we discern the influence of Byron, and also here and there we are reminded of our own standard singers, while "The Old Poet" and the "Legend of the Frauenkirche" bear unmistakable evidences of German style and German influences. We find profound philosophical thoughts scattered through these poems like precious stones set in gold. The apostrophe "To a Cynic" enshrines a deep truth, deeper than we expect to find in the work of a poetess whose cheeks are as yet untouched by the wrinkles of age; and we are forcibly reminded of that verse of

Neue Freie Presse.
1. Februar 1890.

Im englischen Buchhandel ist vor Kurzem ein Bändchen **Gedichte** erschienen, welches beweist, daß es unter unserer praktisch angehauchten Jugend doch noch enthusiastische Seelen gibt, welchen ein Ideal vorschwebt, das sie im Reiche der Poesie zu erlangen hoffen. **Helene Gingold** heißt die jugendliche Dichterin, deren lyrische Gesänge die dritte Auflage erlebt haben. Von Bewunderung für die Dichtung aller Länder erfüllt, ist sie überall zu Hause und besingt mit gleicher Verve und gleichem Schwung ihre eigenen Landsleute, den Rhein, das freie Leben der Zigeuner und überhaupt alles was ihr in den Wurf kommt. Es ist interessant, zu beobachten, wie sich die reelle Welt im Geiste eines zwanzigjährigen Wesens spiegelt. Unter den Mädchen wird es der neuesten Sappho nicht an Freundinnen fehlen.

General-Anzeiger.
5. Juni 1889.

"A Cycle of Verse" ist der Titel eines Buches, dessen Verfasserin Helene E. A. **Gingold** in London sich bereits durch Veröffentlichung anderer Werke bekannt gemacht hat. Das Buch bietet viel Anziehendes und obwohl in englischer Sprache geschrieben, auch Manches, was für deutsche Leser besonders anziehend ist. Bei der Fülle des Gebotenen und der Eleganz der Sprache wird das Werk eine willkommene Gabe sein für Jeden, der an poetisch-literarischen Arbeiten Interesse zeigt. Als die Perlen der Sammlung erscheinen uns "The Wanderer's Farewell to the Rhine," "The Legend of the Frauenkirche in München." Der Anfang "Belcanto" ist eine Arbeit voll guten Humors. Das Titelblatt wird durch das liebliche Portrait der jugend-

"DENYSE,"
A Sketch in Neutral Tints,
By Helene E. A. Gingold.

"GLASGOW HERALD," 1st March, 1883.

This strange but powerful sketch.

"NATAL MERCURY," 11th February, 1890.

Of " Denyse," it may be said that it is a bright, somewhat sentimental, and, on the whole, forcibly-written story. The plot is a common one. A young, passionate and unconventional girl attracts the fancy of a man whose doings are the scandal of the talk, but who is himself the country's idol. Both Denyse and Everard are well-drawn characters, as also is the faithful and dog-like Harold, and the book will pleasantly wile away a spare hour. Its writer will probably make a mark as a tale-writer.

"JEWISH WORLD," 3rd February, 1888.

Her characters are sketched with a light pencil, and with so much vivacity and *entrain* that the reader regrets that the story is brought so soon to a close.

"LONDON AND BRIGHTON," 4th January 1888.

Instead of providing paving material for a future subterranean residence or indulging in senseless toasts, I spent the last hours of the old and the first of the new year in reading

"Denyse," and "Denyse" haunts me still. It may have been the time chosen for reading it, or the unconventionality of the writer, but the book fastens on my mind. Described as a sketch in neutral tints "Denyse" is worth getting by that large class of busy men who like something fresh, but are sick of the orthodox three-volume novel. A Goethe-like *Diabolus*, by Lib on the frontispiece, illustrates the nineteenth chapter, which alone is worth reading. The book is excellently got up, and published by Remington and Co.

"BULLIONIST," 7th January, 1888.

This is a charming volume, brimful of vivacity, and disclosing a rare insight into natural life—its motives and its developments. Denyse Erskyne, the heroine, is an artist of great talent, and distinguished by the inspiration of genius.

"VANITY FAIR," 24th December, 1887.

More of the story we will not tell. Readers are recommended to go for it to the pages of Miss Gingold's very readable novel.

www.ingramcontent.com/pod-product-compliance
Lightning Source LLC
Chambersburg PA
CBHW021808230426
43669CB00008B/679